P9-DFG-672

The

WEEDING

HANDBOOK

ALA Editions purchases fund advocacy, awareness, and accreditation programs for library professionals worldwide.

The

WEEDING

HANDBOOK

A Shelf-by-Shelf Guide

REBECCA VNUK

Booklist collection management editor

An imprint of the American Library Association

CHICAGO | 2015

REBECCA VNUK has a high profile in the library community as a librarian, consultant, workshop presenter, speaker, writer, and blogger. She is currently best known as Editor, Reference and Collection Management, at *Booklist,* and as the co-creator of the popular blog *Shelf Renewal.* Her most recent library position was as Adult Services Director at the Glen Ellyn (IL) Public Library. She has been widely recognized for her contributions to the field. In 2008, she was *Library Journal*'s Fiction Reviewer of the Year, and in 2010 she received the Public Library Association's Allie Beth Martin Award for excellence in Readers' Advisory and was named a *Library Journal* Mover & Shaker. Vnuk is the author of *Read On . . . Women's Fiction* (2009) and *Women's Fiction Authors: A Research Guide* (2009), and co-author (with Nanette Donohue) of *Women's Fiction: A Guide to Popular Reading Interests* (2013). She has spoken at conferences and presented workshops extensively; her panels are among the most popular at ALA Annual and Public Library Association meetings.

© 2015 by the American Library Association

Extensive effort has gone into ensuring the reliability of the information in this book; however, the publisher makes no warranty, express or implied, with respect to the material contained herein.

Printed in the United States of America
19 18 17 16 15   5 4 3 2 1

ISBN: 978-0-8389-1327-7 (paper)

Library of Congress Cataloging-in-Publication Data
Vnuk, Rebecca.
    The weeding handbook : a shelf-by-shelf guide / Rebecca Vnuk.
      pages   cm
    Includes bibliographical references and index.
    ISBN 978-0-8389-1327-7 (pbk. : alk. paper) 1. Discarding of books, periodicals, etc.—Handbooks, manuals, etc. 2. Collection development (Libraries)—United States—Policy statements. 3. Public libraries—Collection development—United States. I. Title.
Z703.6.V68 2015
025.2'16—dc23

        2015008707

Book design by Kimberly Thornton in the Eames, Aleo, and Cardea typefaces.

♾ This paper meets the requirements of ANSI/NISO Z39.48–1992 (Permanence of Paper).

CONTENTS

ACKNOWLEDGMENTS

I MUST ACKNOWLEDGE that this book and the "Weeding Tips" columns in *Booklist* owe a great debt to *CREW: A Weeding Manual for Modern Libraries*. This free publication, originated by Joseph P. Segal and Belinda Boon of the Texas State Library and Archives and updated by Jeanette Larson, is the true bible of weeding and should be obtained and read by every staff member involved in weeding collections. The practical advice in the manual is invaluable, and the shelf-by-shelf layout was a major inspiration for the original "Weeding Tips" columns.

INTRODUCTION

Weeding Skit

Written and performed by Ricki Nordmeyer, Jon Kadus, and Rebecca Vnuk, for the 2000 ALA Annual Conference workshop presented by Merle Jacob, "Weeding the Fiction Collection: Or, Should I Dump *Peyton Place?*"

The three "Weeders" enter the stage with various expressions of agony on their faces and approach a table with several books on it. They have dust masks, latex gloves, a feather duster, and printouts with them.

RICKI. Come on, come on, the sooner we do this the sooner it'll be over!

JON, *looking at his watch*. What time is it?

REBECCA. What else do you have to do?

JON. I select these materials. I'm behind on my journals.

RICKI. We have NO ROOM! You can't purchase more books if there is no space for them.

JON. There's an idea. Why don't they just read the old ones?

REBECCA. Ooh. Look at them. These books are so dirty!

JON. Where? Which One? I must have missed that!

REBECCA. Not that kind of "dirty."

RICKI. That's why I brought these things. (*Distributes masks and gloves; waves around her feather duster.*) We'll clean as we go.

JON. Are these latex? I won't go into prophylactic shock, will I?

REBECCA. That's anaphylactic shock. Little chance of either!

RICKI. OK, OK. Let's get started. What's first?

REBECCA. *Take Leave and Go* by Karel Schoeman. This is like new.

RICKI. It's not in *Fiction Catalog*. When did it last go out?

REBECCA, *checking her printout*. Uh, it's never gone out.

JON. I know I wouldn't have bought it without a great review.

RICKI. It's never gone out!

REBECCA. What if they make it into a movie? I've heard rumors that Spielberg and Gibson want to do this.

RICKI. OK, OK, we'll keep it.

JON. What about this one? *Two Little Misogynists* by Carl Spitteler. It's not in very good shape.

REBECCA. It hasn't gone out since 1987.

RICKI. He won the Nobel Prize for Literature in 1919. We can't discard that, it's an award winner! I know, maybe we'll put it on a display.

JON, *under his breath*. Of oldy-moldy translations?

REBECCA. OK, we have three copies of Jean Paul Sartre's *The Age of Reason*. Can we withdraw this copy?

RICKI. He's definitely in *Fiction Catalog*.

JON. You can never have enough of Sartre!

RICKI. What are the chances of three people in this town wanting this at the same time?

JON. You can never have enough of Sartre!

RICKI. OK, OK . . . What about *The Age of Murderous Snailblasters* by George Salter? It's not in *Fiction Catalog* and I've never heard of the author.

REBECCA. It's never gone out.

JON. Wait a minute! Look at this bookplate.

RICKI. Donated by Hester Stoopover. AGGH!!! The Mayor's wife!

JOHN. You know, I think I pulled this and declared it missing a while back.

REBECCA. She has a stack of them. She just re-donated it.

REBECCA, RICKI and JON, *in unison.* KEEP.

RICKI: *Mayday* by Thomas Block. This was published in 1979.

REBECCA. I was in kindergarten then.

(*Ricki and Jon roll eyes.*)

JON. What time is it? Are we almost done?

REBECCA. What is it? You got a date or something?

JON. As a matter of fact I do.

REBECCA. That must be the first time SINCE I was in kindergarten.

RICKI. All right, all right, back to business here. We have not made any headway, and I'm getting a lot of pressure to do something about these cramped shelves. I think we can pull *Mayday.* Has it ever gone out?

REBECCA. Eighty-two times. It was just returned last week.

JON. Well, that settles that one.

RICKI. Well, I know we'll get rid of this one with the puke-brown library binding . . . *The Women at the Pump* by Knut Hamsun. It's wretched!

JON, *sputtering.* (*Makes up a Norwegian title.*) $#@#$% by Hamsun?? Why, my mother read that to me while I sat on her knee. She would roll over in her grave if she knew I had a part in throwing $#@#$% away. Look! It says it's one of the Foreign Classical Romances right here on the cover.

RICKI. But it's only volume 1 . . .

JON. Then they could get started!!! You just can't throw this away. Why . . .

RICKI and REBECCA, *in unison.* KEEP.

REBECCA. We have twenty-three books by James Fenimore Cooper, but it looks like the only three that have ever circulated are *The Deerslayer, The Last of the Mohicans,* and *The Pathfinder.*

RICKI and JON. But it's Cooper, one of the greatest American authors.

REBECCA. But no one is reading them or cares!

RICKI and JON, *in unison.* JAMES. FENNIMORE. COOPER.

(The two point to the table as Rebecca sadly returns the book to the pile.)

RICKI. Now for a change of pace: We seem to have 1,045 copies of Danielle Steel's books. She is coming out with them monthly now.

JON. YUCK! Get rid of them.

RICKI. You know if we just leave two copies of each that would look like we've weeded an entire range of books.

REBECCA. But it's all in the S's.

JON. Eh, let Circ shift the Steel shelves.

REBECCA. Yeah, Soon it will all be e-books so we won't need to weed.

ALL. We're out of here!!!

Weeding

The very word *weeding* often strikes terror in a librarian's heart. And it's not a new concept: it seems that weeding has been a controversial topic in the field of librarianship for a long time. As Loriene Roy, past President of the American Library Association, and Professor, School of Information, University of Texas at Austin, noted in her entry on weeding in the *Encyclopedia of Library and Information Science,* there were programs on weeding as far back as the 1893 ALA Annual Conference. William Poole, a founding member of ALA, was very concerned that weeding meant a local library would have "no books which will interest persons with an intellectual range above that of clod-hoppers and market gardeners." Melvil Dewey bemoaned that "It is bad enough to stand the critics who complain that a book they wish has not been bought. You can always fall back on lack of funds. But it is a rash librarian who would like to tell one of these gentry that he had recently thrown that very book away."[1]

It's a shame that not much has changed in over 100 years. At just about any library conference, you'll still be able to find a program on weeding. Many librarians have never had formal instruction in weeding—if they were lucky, maybe it was covered in a collection development class (if they took one).

I find no one is ambivalent about weeding—people either love it or loathe it. I fall into the love-it camp. In fact, I once imagined my perfect career would be traveling from library to library across the nation, weeding collections. However, most librarians dread the task. And I'm not heartless; I can see the reasons why. It can be hard to part with books that were carefully selected and paid for with tax dollars. Some librarians feel that it is impossible to imagine that a particular book no longer has any worth. Others have a hard time reconciling their calling as a keeper of information with the need to sometimes discard that information.

All of these worries and doubts are valid, but the bottom line is that libraries (particularly public libraries) are not—and never have been—archives. There simply is not enough space to hang on to every book and every item. And there is no need. A library is an ever-changing organism. Weeding helps a library thrive.

So, what makes me qualified to talk about weeding? In my library career, I've held numerous positions in public libraries, from librarian to collection development specialist to department manager, and in every job I've been in, there was a weeding project. I fell into weeding as a specialty by chance, but I do think that I have the temperament of a weeder. What do I mean by that? I mean that as much as I love reading and am passionate about books, I don't see them as some kind of precious physical item. I don't have an emotional connection to the physical items themselves (even though I have an emotional and intellectual connection to the contents and the authors!).

Like many of my MLIS contemporaries, I didn't have formal weeding instruction in library school. I'm sure it may have been mentioned at some point in my Public Library Administration course, but there was not a lot of time spent on weeding in any of my coursework. A class on collection development wasn't even offered at the time I was on campus. My first encounter with a collection that needed weeding was during an internship at an academic library, where I went to check out a copy of Hesse's *Siddhartha*. The library had a tattered mass-market paperback copy that looked like it was ready for the shredder. The head librarian was, to her credit, quite embarrassed at the condition of the book, especially when I asked her why we couldn't spend the five or so dollars it would cost to buy a replacement.

In my first full-time job out of library school, I worked at a medium-sized suburban library that was tight on space—so tight that at that time, collection development was on a one-bought/one-weeded basis. I was given my first weeding project, which was culling the mystery section. It was an easy task, because we had circulation reports showing what hadn't circulated in the last three years, and I simply used them (and visible condition) as my guideline. Since we spread the project out over several months, and it was obvious to all that we needed space, the project went very smoothly.

My next weeding project was not quite as smooth. In fact, it was a total nightmare. In 2001, the Commissioner of the Chicago Public Library (where I worked as a Collection Development Specialist) deployed a team of librarians to one of the regional branches for a full-scale weeding project. I wasn't involved in the internal politics so I won't get into them here, but suffice it to say that for whatever reason, the collection was badly in need of weeding. Tensions ran high on the project—branch librarians were unhappy that they were not consulted, the branch director was in personal conflict with the Commissioner, and the public was not informed that any such project was going to take place. Because the collection was large, and overdue for weeding, there was a vast number of items removed from the shelves in a short period of time. To cut a long story short, a local alderman was alerted that the library was being "decimated" and decided to head over and see for himself, with a reporter from the neighborhood newspaper in tow. The alderman frightened many of my coworkers by storming into an employees-only workspace, while yelling that our jobs were on the line if we didn't have suitable answers to his questions. Since I was the most senior person in the room, I had the pleasure of dealing with the very irate (and misinformed) gentleman. The incident eventually made it to the *Chicago Tribune,* where I was an "unidentified library official" who ordered the alderman off the premises.[2]

I learned many important lessons from that project. Always—*always*—have staff on board. There is no reason to keep experienced members of your staff from participating in a weeding project. It's also of the utmost importance to keep your community involved in what's going on at the library. (I'll talk more about these two topics in chapter 1, and more about avoiding a weeding disaster in chapter 11.) Looking back, I can certainly see why patrons would be fearful of what was going on. There were recycling bags and Dumpsters filled with what to them appeared to be perfectly useful books. If the public had been better informed about what the project entailed, I have a feeling the entire alderman/reporter incident would have never have occurred.

My next position entailed working at a large suburban library that was preparing to move into a new building. The fiction collection, which I was in charge of, needed to be cut by about 10 percent to prepare for the move. In a three-month period, I single-handedly weeded over 9,000 books. This was TIRING, let me tell you. I would go home, hands aching, and dream at night about books, books, and more books. But it was very rewarding work—the fiction section in the new library building looked fresh and wonderful, and was filled with items that people actually wanted to use. The project went quite smoothly, because we kept our patrons informed of the process and explained to them that the bulk of the items being removed were either multiple copies or items that had not circulated in more than seven years. I don't recall a single patron complaint.

The next major weeding project I was in charge of took place when I worked for a very small suburban public library. The collection was in dire need of a complete overhaul, so we weeded over 45 percent of the entire adult collection. In this instance, I was very lucky that the library's Board also doubled my book budget for a year so that I could replace all of those items! Again, public perception was key—we kept the public informed about why were we getting rid of so much of the collection, and also made them aware of what were we doing to beef it back up. In fact, we kept a "Cart of Shame" during this project, which was instrumental in getting the Board to give us more money for replacements. Nothing beats hard evidence when it comes to illustrating why a weeding project is necessary. No one could argue that it was acceptable to have books on yoga (a trendy topic at the time) that had no photographs but instead had line drawings of poses, or that we needed that softcover book on disco dancing (complete with a pull-out 45 RPM record!). My absolute favorite Cart of Shame item was the particularly nasty Jane Austen omnibus edition. There was something gross and possibly growing on the cover, it smelled like cigarettes, and had the classic wavy pages of something that had been read in the bathtub . . . but we still had it on the fiction shelves. Because, you know, it's really hard to get replacement copies of any Jane Austen titles.

When I took the editing position at *Booklist*, I was put in charge of the e-newsletter *Corner Shelf*, which is devoted to collection development and reader's advisory topics. (You can view issues and subscribe for free at www.booklistonline.com/GeneralInfo.aspx?id=80.) I knew right away that I wanted a recurring feature on weeding. That turned into the popular "Weeding Tips" column, which is the basis for the shelf-specific chapters of this book.

The general weeding guidelines found in the "Weeding Tips" series mainly cover what to get rid of (with a few notes here and there on what can or should remain) from any given library's shelves. And there's good reason for that. I can't tell you exactly what you should keep. In fact, no one can tell you what to keep on your shelves, unless they work with your patrons and your collection. Weeding advice abounds, and much of it relates to a wide range of collections. Reports can guide you in the right direction, but you will actually have to come up with the magic number that works for your library to apply to that data. While it's easy enough to judge most of the nonfiction collection (tell me you don't have outdated medical books on your shelves, please), what's a good length of time to keep a fiction book? Three years with no circulation? Five years? More?

It depends on a variety of issues—how much space do you have? What is your end goal for the weeding project? What condition is the book in? And speaking of condition, who gets to judge? One person's tattered is another's "well-loved" (although I always err on the side of making the grossness factor a big consideration!).

This uncertainly is likely the main reason why some people are so uncomfortable with weeding. We all want reassurance that what we're pulling isn't something that will be needed later. We want to know we've made the right decisions. What helps with those decisions is a solid collection development plan—which is covered in chapter 12. Having a plan in place puts everyone on the same page and can save a lot of time and frustration at all stages of the weeding project. Although it can't tell you what to keep, it can give you firm guidelines of what should—and shouldn't—remain on your shelves.

All of that said, I still fret over the thought of leaving people in the lurch about what to keep and what to weed. Feel free to contact me if you're currently wrestling with something you are unsure about. While I can't claim to give you the definitive, end-all-be-all answer, I may be able to offer some help, or just reassurance that you're on the right track.

How To Use this Book

The goal of this book is to give the reader a good grounding of how and why to weed library collections. I've consciously stayed away from offering numerical formulas, as there are several resources that go in-depth with formulas and statistics. Stanley J. Slotes's *Weeding Library Collections: Library Weeding Methods* offers the idea of a variable called "shelf-time period," defined as the "time a book remains on the shelf between successive uses." Slote's manual espouses that this formula is the best way to create "a smaller core collection that would satisfy a given level of predicted future use."[3] The CREW Manual, which I'll talk about further in chapter 1, offers a numerical formula based on the copyright date, the date of last checkout, and conditional factors.[4]

If you are looking for a formula, then either the Slote Method or CREW will give you what you are looking for. (Some weeders may wish to consult Tony Greiner and Bob Cooper's *Analyzing Library Collection Use with Excel®*.)[5] My aim is to inspire you to weed, and since these publications already offer fantastic suggestions for using numbers and statistics, I'm not going to reinvent the wheel. I encourage readers to peruse the various statistical methodologies available and determine if one would work for their particular collections. My approach is intended to give library staff the knowledge and confidence needed to effectively weed any collection, of any size.

Because this book is intended for public and school libraries, the "shelf-by-shelf" advice is written by Dewey area, not LC. I have made some call-outs in each area for the different considerations of large collections and smaller collections.

A Note on Academic Libraries

Weeding in the academic library could be a separate book altogether, but I didn't want to leave it out of the discussion. While public libraries tend to provide general materials suitable for a variety of users, academic libraries differ in that they need to support the curriculum of the institution. And within the world of academic libraries, a university that supports doctoral candidates requires different materials than a liberal arts college or a community college. More and more often, academic libraries are shifting their budget dollars away from print to electronic resources. So you can see how it would be difficult to talk about academic weeding in general terms.

Many academic libraries seek feedback about the library collection from faculty members, both in terms of what to purchase and what to weed. This gets tricky, because faculty frequently want to keep everything. Or perhaps they were involved in the purchase in the first place, which can make it even more difficult to want to let go of an item. When possible, it is a good idea to give faculty the chance to review items before they are withdrawn, not only as a goodwill gesture, but because faculty may truly be the experts in the subject.

Weeding can also be difficult because many items in an academic library may not circulate. As noted in chapter 1, there are methods that can be used to track non-circulating material, such as asking patrons to tick a piece of paper attached to the front of the book, or asking them not to re-shelve reference items so that at the end of the day, a shelver can make note of items that have been used and left out.

In many academic libraries (and some larger publics), an effort may be made to keep superseded editions or materials that are acknowledged as outdated in order to provide a historical perspective for that discipline. This may not be an issue with the arts and humanities, but is a terrible practice in most other subject fields. Outdated information on medicine, law, and the hard sciences can mislead patrons. An effort should be made to keep such items separate from current materials on a subject, or marked as such.

NOTES

1. Loriene Roy, "Weeding," *Encyclopedia of Library and Information Science,* ed. Allen Kent, Harold Lancour, William Z. Nasri, and Jay Elwood Daily, vol. 54, supplement 17 (New York: Dekker, 1968-), 352-98.

2. Gary Washburn and Rudolph Bush, "City Library Hopes Dispute Is Shelved," *Chicago Tribune,* August 24, 2001, http://articles.chicagotribune.com/2001-08-24/news/0108240230_1_library-issues-library-system-books.

3. Stanley J. Slote, *Weeding Library Collections: Library Weeding Methods,* 4th ed. (Englewood, CO: Libraries Unlimited, 1997).

4. Jeannette Larson, *CREW: A Weeding Manual for Modern Libraries, Revised and Updated* (Austin, TX: Texas State Library and Archives Commission.

5. Tony Greiner and Bob Cooper, *Analyzing Library Collection Use with Excel®*. Chicago: ALA Editions: 2007.

CHAPTER 1

The Basics

LET'S START AT THE BEGINNING: Why is it important that libraries weed?

- **To free up shelf space**
  In most libraries, the shelves should ideally be 75 to 85 percent full. This makes the items much easier to browse, makes it easier to shelve, and, in general, makes the collection look better. But it's not only looks that matter—it also saves the patron time and frustration. When outdated materials are removed, then newer, more frequently used materials become clearly visible on the shelves. Who wants to search through a dozen outdated or ragged books to find the one they are really looking for?
- **Collection development best practices**
  How better to get a good handle on what you already own and what areas you need to beef up than to weed on a regular basis? It can be invaluable to look at and touch every book in your collection. Weeding increases knowledge of the collection as a whole. The selector can see firsthand what materials are damaged, need

updating, or need to be replaced, and also get a sense for what is used (and more importantly when it comes to weeding, what *isn't* used) by the patrons.

- **To purge outdated materials**
  Particularly in nonfiction and in reference, there is a real need to have timely information on your shelves. Remember that your library is not a museum—there is simply not enough space (nor is it a library's mission) to be a warehouse of unused books. It's also very important to remember that reference material has an expiration date!

Crowded shelves and worn-out books are distasteful, especially to busy patrons. Just as a bookstore will clearance out titles that do not sell to make room for the constant arrival of new books to keep an eye on profits, a library must consider if removing titles that do not circulate may maintain or even increase its budget allocation. How does that work? The budget is often set in relation to the value and esteem in which the community holds the library, which in turn depends to a large degree on circulation figures.

The idea that we are the chosen keepers of the sacred books is at odds with the fact that weeding actually goes to the very core of the librarian's professional responsibility to offer patrons the very best information possible. To those librarians who feel that weeding goes against what we have been called to do; our duty to protect books and information: I would remind them of the last two of S. R. Ranganathan's Five Laws of Library Science: *Save the time of the reader* and *The library is a growing organism*.

Ideally, weeding is an ongoing process. Many libraries try to follow a weeding schedule that allows for an easy, continual flow to the weeding process. Weeding throughout the year reduces the number of materials withdrawn at one time and keeps your community happy—because the shelves look fresh, and patrons will not see a large number of books leaving the building at one given time. If you haven't made an effort to weed continually—or even if you have—oftentimes a weeding project may be needed. Specifically, you know you need a "deep weed" when shelf space becomes impossible to navigate or patrons complain about the condition of materials or a lack of current information.

Weeding Responsibility

One thing you may or may not choose to designate in a collection development plan is who is actually responsible for weeding the collection. Because few libraries, especially smaller ones, have a dedicated collection development librarian, your collection development plan should spell out the personnel in each department who are responsible for weeding. The best way to handle this is to let those who select materials also be responsible for deselecting them. These staff members should have the expertise and experience with their collection areas, and therefore would be able to make good decisions. Personal and detailed knowledge of the collection can be indispensable when weeding. In addition, first-hand knowledge about the community and the tastes of local users comes in handy. If one person handles all of the materials buying (as is common in smaller libraries), then a committee or group should be formed to cover weeding. Team weeding lessens the burden, and provides for a balanced view of the collection. Final decisions should rest with department managers (or the library director). This should be clearly stated in the collection development plan.

Where to Begin?

You'll see this again in chapter 12: Have a solid collection development plan in place. This not only gives you backup by highlighting your reasons for weeding and your timeline, but also gives your staff instruction. On page 16, I offer a basic, easily adaptable sample to kickstart the weeding and retention section of a collection development plan.

There are a number of ways to handle the question of *when* to weed. Many libraries rely on automated computer reports to identify low-circulating items. It's easy enough to have those items pulled, reviewed, and decided upon. Some libraries specify (by policy or when space necessitates) that a certain percentage of the collection must be evaluated on an annual basis. There are less formal ways of accomplishing weeding tasks as well, such as having librarian selectors periodically check their areas or have shelvers alert them to overcrowded areas that need weeding. I feel very strongly that all libraries can benefit from having a published schedule for weeding.

A wonderful example of a weeding schedule comes from King County Library System in Washington. KCLS uses the following schedule as a guideline for weeding collections, aimed at a review of the entire collection each year (reprinted with permission).

January	000–099		July	500–599
January	Fiction A-B		July	Fiction N-O-P
January	Youth Graphic Novels		July	ABE/ESL
February	100–199		August	600–699
February	Fiction C-D-E		August	Fiction Q-R
February	J Series		August	Reference
March	200–299		September	700–799
March	Fiction F-G		September	Fiction S
March	World Language		September	Audiobooks (including read-alongs)
April	300–399		October	800–899
April	Fiction H-I-J		October	Fiction T-U-V
April	E/J Folk and Fairy Tales		October	E Readers
May	400–499		November	900–999
May	Fiction K-L		November	Fiction W
May	DVDs		November	Teen Classics
June	Fiction M		December	Fiction X-Y-Z
June	Large Print		December	Biographies
June	CD Music		December	E Board Books

All major integrated library system (ILS) software has the ability to generate circulation reports. You may be able to run them yourself, or you may have to request them from your vendor, but the records exist—use them! Reports available from your cataloging system are invaluable for weeding. You can sort them by all kinds of criteria, including last checkout date, age of item, and number of checkouts. The numbers will, of course, vary depending on the size and type of library and the intent of your collection, but chapters 2 through 9 offer some general advice. Reports can give you a great overall picture of your collection, even outside of the numbers specific to each item. For example, a report can show you the average circulation rate of items at a particular call number. This will let you know whether you need to take a closer look at the section, or if you need to purchase more in that area, for example.

Pre-Weeding Steps

- **Identify Stakeholders:** Library administrators need to support and endorse the weeding process. Librarians need to be prepared to weed. Support staff, such as shelvers or IT personnel, may be called upon to create lists and check for circulation of weeded materials not on the lists. Catalogers and other technical services staff will need to assist with updating holdings and the discard process.
- **Shelf Read:** This will ensure that the area to be worked on is complete and allows you the opportunity to check what may be missing or lost from the collection.
- **Pull Visibly Damaged Items:** A page or shelver can perform a quick run-through of shelves due for weeding, and pull items that need a closer look purely based on condition.
- **Build Weeding into the Schedule:** When staff have a clear understanding of a project, they are more likely to get it done in a reasonable amount of time. Schedule time for weeding the same way you would schedule on-desk hours.
- **Determine Your Steps:** There are important questions to consider. Will you work a literal shelf at a time? Will you work in the stacks

or move a truck to the workroom? What will you do with items that need replacing or mending? Where will discards go?

Things to Look For

- outdated information (particularly in the 300s and 600s)
- outdated Popular Interest
- repetition or multiple copies
- superseded editions
- tattered or dirty items
- poorly bound items
- dated dust jackets (especially in Youth collections)
- little use or lack of patron demand
- no long-term or historical significance
- space limitations/oversaturation in certain areas

The *CREW Method* (which stands for **C**ontinuous **R**eview, **E**valuation, and **W**eeding), created by Belinda Boon and Joseph P. Segal, offers six general guidelines for judging library material under the acronym MUSTIE. (For more information, see www.tsl.state.tx.us/ld/pubs/crew):

- M = *misleading:* factually inaccurate
- U = *ugly:* beyond mending or rebinding
- S = *superseded* by a new edition or by a much better book on the subject
- T = *trivial:* of no discernible literary or scientific merit
- I = *irrelevant* to the needs and interests of the library's community
- E = *elsewhere:* the material is easily obtainable from another library

Other common acronyms include WIDUS: (Weed Us!) **W**orn out, **I**nappropriate, **D**uplicated, **U**ncirculated, **S**uperseded; and WORST: **W**orn out, **O**ut of date, **R**arely used, **S**upplied elsewhere, **T**rivial or faddish.

It may sound trite, but don't be afraid to weed on looks alone. I've been in too many libraries where a good one-third of the collection could be replaced based on rips, smells, and stains alone. Who wants to check out a nasty book? This can be an easy way to weed on an ongoing basis. Ask the circulation staff to hold questionable books that are returned to the library. Coach your shelvers on how to preselect tattered materials for a librarian to check.

Wesleyan University completed a massive weeding project from 2011 through 2014, culling some 60,000 volumes from the collection. Staff detailed the project from start to finish on their blog "WesWeeding," (http://weeding.blogs.wesleyan.edu). One entry to the blog detailed their criteria for setting up initial lists of books to withdraw (reprinted with permission).

Criteria Used in the Creation of the Potential Withdrawal Lists

1. **Books published before 1990:** Many—not all—scholarly books are most useful, and most used, in the several years just after they are published. Books that are over 20 years old are less likely to be used and are therefore good candidates for weeding.

2. **Books added to the library's collection before 2003:** Books added to the library's collections recently may prove useful, but have not been in the collection long enough to be proved useful or otherwise. We are retaining books added since 2003 so that they have more time to be discovered and used. Why 2003? In 2003 the library migrated to our current online library system, and we know what books we ordered before and after 2003. So 2003 is a convenient breakpoint for this criterion.

3. **Books that have not checked out since 2003, and have checked out once or not at all since 1996:** Books with one or fewer checkouts since 1996, and none since 2003, may be of less use to students and faculty than books that have checked out more frequently during the same time period. Why 2003 and 1996? As noted above, 2003 is when we migrated to our current online system, and we have detailed circulation statistics for each book since then. We have summary circulation statistics for each book from 1996 to 2002, when we were using a different online system. Before then we do not have online circulation statistics.

4. **Books held by more than 30 other libraries in the United States:** If a withdrawn book is later needed by a Wesleyan student or faculty member, we will order it through interlibrary loan (ILL). Books held by more than 30 other libraries in the U.S. will be easy to find and order via ILL.

(continued)

5. **Books held by two or more partner libraries:** Wesleyan University Library is part of the CTW Consortium, with Trinity College and Connecticut College. The CTW Consortium, with the library at the University of Connecticut at Storrs, share collections through a delivery service. We can be confident that books held by two or more of our partners in this service will be quickly available if needed by a Wesleyan student or faculty member.

How We Combined These Criteria (For Fans of Boolean Logic)

The books on the list of potential withdrawals meet all of these criteria. So, they are published before 1990 AND added to the collections before 2003 AND have not checked out since 2003 AND have checked out once or not at all since 1996 AND are held by more than 30 libraries in the US AND are held by two or more of our partner libraries.

If a book does not meet all these criteria, it is not on the list.

Reprinted with permission from http://weeding.blogs.wesleyan.edu/page/3.

What if you just aren't sure about a particular title? Ask yourself the following questions:

- Would I be embarrassed if the library didn't own it?
- Does the book fit the needs of my community?/Does it have local interest?
- Is the author still living and writing?
- If I put this on display, would it go out?

There's an excuse for everything, and here are some rebuttals to the things that may be keeping you from weeding:

- *That's taxpayer money!* It's more of a waste of taxpayer dollars to keep outdated or nasty books on the shelf. Time is money, too—your patrons shouldn't have to waste their time searching through your outdated collections.
- *But I bought that book myself—I have a personal connection to it!* Think of your personal responsibility to the collection as a whole.
- *Books are valuable!* There is no value in dangerously outdated material or soiled items.

- *I'm afraid it will look bad to have empty shelves.* Keep your community informed about what's happening when you weed, and remember that replacement is a key component of weeding as well.
- *This is someone's favorite book!* And we'd be happy to ILL it for him.

Getting Staff On Board

All staff members, whether they are directly involved in the weeding process or not, should be made aware of the task at hand. It's important to keep all library staff informed so they can alleviate any patron anxieties. Front-line staff are the ones who work with the collection on a daily basis, and they are the ones who discuss what's happening with concerned patrons. Staff who are directly involved need to be part of the process, and should have input. There needs to be an understanding, if not an agreement, on exactly what is going to happen to the collection: why the weeding project needs to take place and how it's going to work.

Staff members who are given responsibility for purchasing should also be responsible for weeding. It's simply part of the collection development cycle. Librarians who select in an area should have the professional judgment to know when to cull and to update.

It's important to remember that everyone in the library has a stake in weeding, and will likely be called upon to assist. Therefore it is crucial that the entire staff understands what needs to happen and how it's going to happen. All library staff need to stay informed so they can alleviate any patron anxieties. If staff is not on board with weeding, your public will never be.

Public Perception

Talking about weeding shouldn't be secretive or become a painful process. Staff should use positives instead of negatives when talking about it, and should never complain to patrons about the bad materials that were on the shelf previously. (The one exception to this is using the Cart of Shame to your advantage, as mentioned below on page 13.) Instead, they can explain that the library is making room for new materials, making the shelves easier to navigate, and replacing outdated information with current information. In fact, it's important for everyone to keep in mind that weeding isn't always about clearing the shelves—sometimes it's about getting fresh new copies of the exact same titles. More on the subject of public perception is discussed in chapter 11.

Frequently Asked Questions about Weeding

In the weeding workshops and webinars I give, many of the same questions pop up over and over again. Here they are, complete with answers.

What can we do with weeded copies?

Depending on what your library's policies or restraints may be, there are a number of ways to clear out weeded copies. (Academic and school libraries in particular need to check with their administration to make sure they are following proper procedures, and some municipalities may have rules about disposal of "public property." Although I have never come across this myself, it's a very good idea to cover all bases and check first!)

Sell
- Sell discarded items that have been properly readied (remove barcodes and labels, black out library stamps if desired) at library book sales—ongoing or events.
- Sell online via Powell's (www.powells.com/sell); B-logistics (www.blogistics.com/); eBay (www.ebay.com); Amazon Marketplace (http://sellercentral.amazon.com). Consider rounding up volunteers or asking your Friends groups for assistance, so that it doesn't take up too much staff time.

Give Away

- I implore you: only give away items that are in good condition and up to date. If you don't want these items, do you think another library really does? If you are discarding items in good condition, such as multiple copies, contact local schools or nearby libraries. You can also check with Libraries of Love, a registered nonprofit that works to create libraries in African schools (www.libraries oflove.org/). In addition, ALA has a great fact sheet on "Sending Books to Needy Libraries" that can be found at www.ala.org/tools/ libfactsheets/alalibraryfactsheet12.

Recycle

- Are there special local recycling days in your area? Does your library have the funds to temporarily rent more recycling bins (this option is probably not as expensive as you may think).
- Use a service such as Better World Books (www.betterworldbooks .com). They'll pay for pickup; you can donate the books and designate a charity for the profits to go to, or they will sell and give you a percentage of the money. There is a similar service called Bookforward (www.bookforward.net), which sells via Amazon.
- The Austin (TX) Public Library has a website devoted to "green weeding" (http://library.austintexas.gov/green-weeding). Its goal is to raise awareness of carbon-neutral options to deal with books and materials being weeded and discarded from library collections, and to keep books and other media out of landfills. They do this by selling items at their bookstore, Recycled Reads, and exploring recycling options.

Finally, don't be afraid to recognize that books will just have to go in the trash, like it or not. No one has a use for moldy, smelly, or damaged books.

Do we need to keep every award-winning book?

Absolutely not, if it's not circulating. If you have a damaged copy and the item is still in demand, then it's a great candidate for replacement. Lists of award-winners can be useful for collection development but I will state that I never feel that a list of award-winners or an index supersedes common sense and local knowledge.

We have a professor who is adamant about keeping all of the books in his subject area, even though they do not circulate. What do we do?

If you've shown him circulation reports and he won't budge, then why not put the onus on him—if he wants them to be kept, he needs to find storage space for them in his office or his department.

What do we need to do about gift books and books by local authors?

Ideally, you will have a statement in your collection development plan that covers this (see chapter 12 for more detail on such a statement). There is no reason that a library must keep items that were donated or that were authored by locals, though it stands to reason that if there is room in the collection, it is a nice gesture to keep items by local writers.

In a library without subject experts, how do we identify the classic or landmark books in a subject that we would want to keep? Or should it not even be a consideration?

As noted above, while indexes and catalogs can be useful as a starting point or as justification for keeping items, I caution librarians not to use such lists blindly. Be sure to keep your patrons and your mission in mind when making choices for your collection. That said, for a situation such as this, it may be helpful to consult *Wilson's Public Library Catalog*. (The newest edition has been split into *Public Library Core Collection: Nonfiction* and *Public Library Core Collection: Fiction*.) It's a good starting point for non-subject specialists.

My staff members do not want to weed ANYTHING. Help!

Sometimes tough love is necessary. Micromanage, and make staff justify keeping items. For example, if staff insist they need several different sets of similar books, I would pull a couple of them, put them in storage or the staff workroom, and then make staff tell me when they last actually used them and for what. Could they have used something else? It sounds silly, and as I said, it's micromanaging, but with some people, that's what you have to do.

Can you learn to love weeding?

If you need to learn to love weeding, you can help yourself by attending conference programs and webinars, reading articles, and, really, looking at the results from your weeding. Also, weed slowly and small, and weed as you go along—then it won't seem so destructive or overwhelming.

If a book is ten years old and hasn't circulated recently, is giving it one last chance (on an endcap or display) justified?

Absolutely—if you have the display space, and it's not outdated information, go ahead and give it one last chance. You never know what might catch someone's eye. If it doesn't go out, then you know you were right to pull it.

How do you maintain fiction series or complete collections of an author's work?

I do feel that if the author is still popular or still writing, it is important to keep series intact. You should decide either to keep them all or get rid of them all—don't weed book five of a series just because that's the one with the least circs. See chapter 7 for more information on weeding series.

How do you justify weeding to patrons when they complain that your budget is going up?

Transparency is key—a "Cart of Shame" works well to illustrate why you're getting rid of materials. Show her the badly outdated, moldy, and damaged books. The Cart of Shame is, literally, a bookcart you use to store some of your worst discards. Showing people the things you are weeding can be quite effective. I've used a Cart of Shame to show staff, boards, and patrons the following:

- *The Mongoloid Child: Recognition and Care* (1977). Can you imagine a parent of a child with Down Syndrome coming across this book when seeking out resources at the public library? I was horrified when I took this off the shelf.
- A book on housekeeping, circa 1960, which extolled the virtues of having a dishwasher, which would allow the "lucky housewife" to have so much free time!
- A 1978 title on disco dancing, which included a never-used tear-out vinyl record. I actually thought this was a joke item.
- My all-time favorite, the omnibus of Jane Austen titles that was so filthy and disgusting that I had to put it in a sealed plastic bag before putting it on the Cart. It was amazing that anyone would have thought it was appropriate to keep on the shelf, particularly when you consider that just about every Austen title is still in print and very inexpensive to replace!

For more examples, you simply must visit AwfulLibraryBooks.net. Librarians Holly Hibner and Mary Kelly feature examples of actual books recently weeded from library collections, and they range from humorous to horrific. You can learn more about the site and about Hibner and Kelly in an interview I conducted with them for *Booklist* (www.booklistonline.com/Notes-from-the-Field-Talking-about-Awful-Library-Books-with-Holly-Hibner-and-Mary-Kelly-Rebecca-Vnuk/pid=6139204).

Our mystery titles go out many times a year and are, by and large, in good shape. But we need space. So how do I know what to weed? Similar question: How do you weed collections that continue to circulate—such as audiobooks and DVDs—so that you can make room for new acquisitions and requests?

It's a tough call when your patrons are using the materials and they are in good condition. If it's a space issue and not a use condition, you might need to tighten up how long you're willing to go between checkouts. Some smaller libraries use three years as a benchmark. It's not unusual to go down to two—but even I will admit that's getting harsh. Think about whether there is any chance you could weed a less-used area and expand the tight section.

Do you know of any research on patron attitudes toward a book's condition? We may call them ugly, but do our patrons think so, or are we projecting?
More often than not, it's the patrons who have a more critical eye! Librarians tend to be a lot more forgiving of condition than patrons. You know it's bad when a patron worries at the circ desk about taking something home because they don't want to be blamed for the condition the book is in. You can certainly also use a more positive term, such as "worn out" or "well used," rather than "ugly."

What do you recommend the number of checkouts should be for an item before weeding? For example, I have weeded items that have very old publication dates but had one or two checkouts in 2012.
In a case like this (old material but recent checkouts), it depends on condition and relevancy of information. If it's fiction, you can feel fine keeping it (or replacing it if it's tattered). If it's nonfiction, weigh the accuracy and currency of the material.

I am new to the job and the only person weeding the collection. Any suggestions on how to divide it up so that I am not overwhelmed?
Go section by section so that you are able to concentrate on one area at a time. Look to the "Weeding Tips" series on *Booklist Online* and the CREW Manual, both of which go through the Dewey areas shelf by shelf.

Sample Weeding Guidelines

While many libraries mention weeding in their collection development plans or policies (see chapter 12), it's usually best to leave the nuts-and-bolts to an internal document that staff can use as a guideline while they work.

The following guidelines were written for a suburban library with a collection of 100,000–150,000 volumes. They are meant as a generic document for an average collection. Feel free to adapt them to fit the needs of your library, based on the size of your collection and usage reports.

Retention and Weeding

Retention is based on the likelihood of a historical interest in the field as well as the timeliness of a title and its informational content. Patron demand also has an impact on the retention or replacement of material.

While we document a minimum schedule for weeding below, it is important to note that weeding is done on an ongoing basis as needed, to make room for newer titles and when materials that are in poor condition come to our attention.

Specific timetables for different sections of the collection are detailed in this plan. In general, the schedule is as follows:

> *Annually*: 000-Computers, Large Print, Adult Mass Market
>   Paperbacks, 900-Travel
> *Biennially*: 300-Legal, College, Investment, Medical
> *Every three years*: Reference, 000, 100s, 500s, 600s, AV
> *Every five years*: Fiction, 300s, 700s
> *Every six years*: 200s, 400s, 800s, 900s, Biography

Multiple copies will be purchased to meet patron demand. After initial demand has passed, most duplicate copies will be removed from the collection.

Fiction

The fiction collection should be evaluated and weeded every five years. Once an individual title is no longer popular, the library should not retain more than two copies of a specific title. Titles that have not circulated for seven years will be considered for weeding.

Nonfiction Circulating Collection
Once an individual title is no longer popular, the library should not retain more than one copy of it. With a few exceptions, the library will retain only the current edition of a title.

000—Generalities
Because of rapid changes in this field, the computer collection will be weeded at least annually. Other titles in the area should be evaluated every three years. Titles that have not circulated in five years will be considered for weeding.

100—Philosophy and Psychology
Special emphasis will be placed on self-help materials, which will be weeded every three years to maintain currency, and topics in demand for school assignments, which will be weeded every four years.

200—Religion
Information in this area is usually not time sensitive; therefore weeding of this area should be every six years. Titles that have not circulated in five years will be considered for weeding.

300—Social Sciences
Current information is crucial in this area. Tax guides are kept for seven years. Multiple copies are weeded out after the current tax year. The college guides and test preparation books are kept up-to date by standing order plans. Titles in the legal, personal investment, colleges guide and test preparation areas need to be evaluated every two years, and will be considered for weeding if they have not circulated in three years. All other areas should be weeded every five years. Titles with the exceptions noted above will be considered for weeding if they have not circulated for five years.

400—Language
This area should be evaluated every six years, and titles that have not circulated for five years will be considered for weeding.

500—Science
This area should be weeded every three years. Titles that have not circulated in five years will be considered for weeding.

600—Applied Science and Technology
This area needs to be evaluated and weeded every two years. Currency of information is particularly important in this area of the collection, and in general materials over five years old will be weeded. The rest of this collection will be weeded on a rotating cycle, each section evaluated every three years.

700—Arts
This collection should be weeded every five years. Titles that have not circulated in five years will be considered for weeding.

800—Literature
Information in this area is usually not time sensitive; therefore weeding of this area should be every six years. Titles that have not circulated in five years will be considered for weeding.

900—History
Information in this area is usually not time sensitive; therefore weeding of this area should be every six years. Titles that have not circulated in five years will be considered for weeding.

910-919—Travel
Travel guides are kept up-to date by standing order plans, and guides that are published annually will be weeded every two to three years.

Biographies
This area should be weeded every six years. Titles that have not circulated in five years will be considered for weeding.

Large Print
Due to space considerations, the collection should be evaluated and weeded every year.

Adult Mass Market Paperbacks
Paperbacks will be weeded continuously, although tattered copies with high circulation will be reordered for the collection.

Databases and Electronic Resources
An essential consideration in retaining online database products is patron use. Subscription databases that do not show substantial use (considering the cost of the product) over a year's time will be replaced or removed.

Audiovisual Collection
All AV collections will be weeded on an as-needed basis, and titles that have not circulated in three years will be considered for weeding. Items in poor condition are evaluated and removed from the collection or replaced if warranted.

Periodicals and Newspapers
Titles are kept for varying lengths of time, though the majority are retained for the current plus three years. Usage is continually evaluated, and titles not used are weeded so that new periodicals may be acquired. A patron survey may be done on individual titles on an as-needed basis, with a comprehensive survey completed at least once every five years.

CHAPTER 2

Shelf by Shelf: 000, 100, 200

et's start at the beginning of the collection (with apologies to LC collections!). I find that the 000s tend to be difficult to weed, mainly due to the wildly varying nature of the books. On the one hand, this section contains computer books, which should turn over fairly rapidly. But it also contains encyclopedias—if you still have them, that is—and general trivia-type books. Weeding the 100s should be a fairly easy task, since the material holds up well, and there isn't a great deal of new or superseded information constantly being published on philosophy. Religion is also not a particularly difficult section, as long as you know what your community needs and keep a good mix of titles.

004 / Computers

In most cases, out-of-date titles should not be retained, even if nothing else is available on that subject in the collection. Here's where it gets tricky for most librarians. You want to keep all of those Word 2003 books on the shelf, don't you? You just know that you still have patrons who use that program, even though it's ten years out of date and has been superseded by two updates. (Hey, I'm not one to judge—up until recently, Office 2003 was my choice on my home computers since I was used to it!) But how likely is it that your patrons will need books on that program? After all, if they still have the program, they have likely had it for many years, and it's certainly not difficult to locate user guides and tips online. It's reasonable to keep books on software programs dating one release back, but no further. If you must keep books on outdated computer programs, winnow it down to one copy and one title per program. Trust me.

010 / Bibliography

Bibliographies and readers' advisory tools are fine to keep if they are in good condition and were published within the last ten years. Consider weeding if they have not circulated in the last three years. *Larger collections: Consider weeding if they have not circulated in the last five years.*

020 / Library Science

Unless you are near a university with a library science program, there's really no sense in keeping most of your library-related books on the public shelves. Find a space in the staff area for them, and discard all material that is obsolete or outdated.

030 / Encyclopedias

I'm almost afraid to talk about print encyclopedias here, for I don't want to incur the wrath of print-loving librarians everywhere. But I think it's time to face up to the fact that general print encyclopedias are no longer the way to go. If you have a set that is more than three years old, it's time to send it packing—unless you are in a school library and can honestly say you have seen—with your own eyes—students using them. Older sets can circulate, but I'd be wary of information over eight years old. Naturally, specialized encyclopedias that are updated irregularly should be retained until a new edition is available, but those are likely shelved in their respective Dewey sections. *Larger collections: Consider circulating a superseded set if the new edition resides in Reference.*

Other 000s

Go ahead and keep most trivia books and quotation books as long as you have the room and they are being used. In the case of *The Guinness Book of World Records, Farmers' Almanac,* and similar titles, keep the current edition and one previous edition. In addition, in most libraries titles of this nature can be moved to the circulating shelves.

100 / Philosophy

Although it's true that most philosophy books will not become outdated, if the books aren't circulating, it's time to weed them out after three years of not circulating. Do keep a selection of titles that cover Western and Asian philosophies. *Larger collections: Keep books that are in good shape, weed after five years of no circulation.*

130 / Occult, Paranormal, Dream books

This shelf is likely fairly self-weeding, with a high rate of use and an equally high rate of theft, loss, and damage. Books on witchcraft, dream interpretation, and astrology are easy (and relatively inexpensive) to replace, so weed based on usage and appearance.

150 / Psychology

While the classics of psychology can remain on the shelves based on popularity and use, pop psychology and self-help books need a frequent weed. Keep an eye on titles that are no longer popular, and don't bother holding on to celebrity books for more than a few years. In general, you should consider weeding self-help books that have a copyright older than five years, and weed those that have not circulated in the past three years.

160 / Logic
170 / Ethics and Morality

Discard worn-out classics in the field and replace with new editions where possible. Examine the books in the 170s for outdated outlooks or moral values, particularly on hot-button topics such as euthanasia or sexuality. Moral choices and decisions change drastically from generation to generation, even over the span of a few years. Be sure the items in this area represent current thinking and trends.

200 / Religion and Mythology

It can feel difficult to weed books on religion, because you might not want to offend anyone or be accused of favoritism. But if you have something current on each of the major international religions—Buddhism, Christianity, Hinduism, Islam, Judaism, and Taoism—you're well covered. Add Scientology and sects such as Amish, Mennonite, and others as space and interest allow. Although the ideas in religious writings do not tend to go out of date, they do reflect the periods in which they were written, and their language becomes dated, so it's useful to weed on a ten-year cycle. If a work implies that is a reflection of "contemporary" religious thought, it needs to have been published within the last ten years. Keep classics by famous theologians as long as they are popular and in good condition. Mythology is usually of great interest to students, so keep several copies of the popular works on hand.

CHAPTER 3

Shelf by Shelf: 300s

L et's continue our look at weeding your collection with the Dewey 300s. This is a tricky section, due to the sheer range of topics—politics, sociology, crime, education, and folklore are all found here. The best bet is to dice up the 300s into manageable sections, rather than try to look at it as a whole. Some areas can stay relatively unchanged, while others need a strict schedule of replacement for timeliness. Some of the most controversial topics are found in the 300s, so a careful evaluation for current, balanced topics is a must. It may be very useful to apply a team-weeding approach to some sections of the 300s, for balance and to break up the workload.

300 / Social Sciences, Sociology and Anthropology

One of the things I've noticed when weeding various collections is that the 300s—particularly 300-309—end up with books dropped here and there, depending on when they were acquired and who was cataloging. The 305 and 306 areas seem to be particularly tricky, thanks to the way they break down—Men and Women, Women, Sexual Relations, and Marriage and Family are each at different classifications between 305 and 306. In some libraries, this can mean the items are multiple shelves away from each other. My standard advice here is to take the opportunity, while weeding, to reclassify items as needed. Go with what makes sense for the size and scope of your collection, and remember that what you're aiming for here is to get the book in the hands of the patron, whether or not that follows a strict interpretation of classification rules.

In general, books on society and culture should be evaluated every three years or so, with an eye toward current subjects and amount of use. Carefully evaluate books on Black History, Women's Issues, and Gender for language and bias.

310 / Statistics

Databooks and statistics need frequent weeding—keep only the current volume and one previous edition. Since current census information is available online, you can feel comfortable weeding print copies unless you see an actual need for them at your particular institution.

320 / Political Science

Unless your library specializes in political history, weed out any information that is no longer relevant to current political campaigns. For books on current political topics, weed within three years of copyright date. Here's another chance to reorganize your collection: Do you have similar items in the 900s? You also need to keep an eye out for bias in this section—it can be difficult for selectors to stay on top of point-counterpoint titles, and because we're only human, everyone leans toward one side or the other. You may not ever get to a place of equal balance, but do try to keep opposing sides in mind.

General guides to the political process, histories of political parties, or the electoral system may be kept longer, and weeded on the basis of use. Books on civil rights remain popular with students and general readers, so weed and replace based on usage and condition.

Immigration and citizenship guides are also found here, but make sure you are not duplicating what you might have in an ESL or ELL collection. Update study guides for citizenship tests as new editions become available—you should have fresh items published within the last three years. The United States citizenship test went through a major overhaul in 2008, so you absolutely need to weed anything published prior to that year.

330 / Economics

Your basic books on personal finance should be updated frequently and weeded based on usage and condition. Real estate and money management are two topics that quickly become dated, so a constant turnover of items is to be expected. A book published even ten years ago is woefully out of date as far as wages and living expenses go, so aim for a ten-year copyright cutoff in personal finance. Books on careers and job hunting also need frequent weeding and replacement with updated items; again, a ten-year copyright cutoff should be standard here.

Tax books seem to be something that librarians don't want to get rid of, and I can't quite understand why. Yes, it's true that individuals should keep tax returns for seven years, but trust me, if your patron is still dealing with their taxes from 2005, they are not likely coming to the library for information, they're consulting a tax attorney! In my opinion, there is no need for most public libraries to keep older tax guides, just keep the current guide and previous two years' editions, maximum. *Larger collections may wish to keep guides going back seven years if there is a usage demand.*

Classic titles in the field of economics can be kept or replaced as usage warrants.

340 / Law

Law books actually are not as hard as they seem—replace personal law books, guides, and reproducible forms as new editions come out, which is likely on an annual or biannual basis. Do not keep outdated editions. Look at your circulation figures to determine relevant topics for your community—divorce, real estate, wills. It's not a bad idea to keep duplicate items of basic law guides, particularly the compilations of reproducible forms, in your reference section.

Code books specific to your area belong in the reference section, but check to see what is currently available online. It's highly unlikely you will need to be a source of historical code information, so do not keep outdated editions.

General guides on finding an attorney or the basics of the legal system can be kept based on usage and appearance, as well as books that examine the history of major legal cases. LSAT study guides for law school should not be kept longer than three years—the test was last revised in 2007, so you should absolutely weed any items before that date.

350 / Public Administration and Military Science

Most of what you find here can be weeded on a five-year basis, with the exception of civil service or military entrance test guides, which should be updated every three years.

360 / Social Services

This is a broad section where it is easy to get bogged down. In the 360s, it's most comfortable to weed in bite-size areas. Hot topics, such as addictions, end-of-life issues, environmental issues, and social problems, should be weeded on currency (no more than two to five years old, max) as well as usage. Many students use books from this section when writing reports on drugs or alcohol. Substances that are used (and abused) change over time, and new drugs become "trendy" (for lack of a better term), so it's important to weed out outdated information here.

Books that focus on disabilities or coping with major illnesses need to be scrutinized for outdated terminology and treatment options. Once again, this is the time to check against what you also have in the 600s. Titles by cancer survivors are often found at 362 as well as 616 (and possibly in with your biographies)—is that really helpful for your readers?

True crime, which tends to be popular, should be weeded on appearance and as usage wanes. Replace popular and classic works. Forensic-science titles should be weeded as techniques are updated and interests change.

370 / Education

College guides and entrance-exam books should be weeded and replaced as frequently as usage warrants. Very few items should be kept more than five years. A quick online search will tell you when major tests were last updated.

Books on the theory and practice of education should be weeded every seven to ten years, and this is a good opportunity to collaborate with your local school administration and teachers—they might know best what is relevant and important.

380 / Commerce, Communications and Transportation

Quick check: Where are your books on railroads? In this section or at 625? Let's hope they're not in both. Another chance to reorganize your collection lies in the narrow 380s. Many titles here will also be found scattered elsewhere—if you have a consortial catalog, it might be interesting to see where other libraries put some of these titles. In general, this is not an area where things change rapidly (with the exception of communications), so it's safe to weed on a five-year rotation, with your focus on usage.

390 / Customs, Etiquette, Holidays, and Folklore

Wedding-planning and holiday-celebration books can be weeded based on usage and condition and frequent replacement should occur as trends change. Weed out celebrity books as popularity wanes.

Etiquette books are classic and can be weeded based on usage and condition. Do keep on top of new editions, and don't bother keeping superseded editions.

Holiday books should be evaluated for timeliness and attractiveness. Are they diverse? Does the book look appealing? While the content may not need to be updated (unless you have books here on decorating and entertaining—or are they in your 700s where they belong?), the appeal factor is a big consideration.

Fairy tales and folklore do not go out of date, so feel free to weed here based on usage and condition. It gets interesting, though, when one looks at the quality of the retelling, especially in older editions if ethnic or racial concerns are present. Replace classic collections with new and attractive editions. *Larger collections may be weeded more on condition than on usage history, if space allows.*

CHAPTER 4

Shelf by Shelf: 400s and 500s

Atter slogging through the long and often unwieldy 300s, it feels good to know that the 400s and 500s are some of the easiest-to-weed parts of a collection. It helps that, in most public libraries, the 400s and 500s are also the smallest parts of the collection.

The Criteria For the 400s (Language)

This can almost exclusively rest on usage and condition. The field of languages and linguistics is stable and not particularly time-sensitive. And if you have plenty of space, don't even worry much about your usage statistics. Some items, such as dictionaries, will be more readily used in the library rather than checked out, so you can keep those—if you have room and they are in good condition—even if your checkout numbers are low. If budget allows, replace English dictionaries and grammar classics when new editions are released.

Foreign language and English as a Second Language (ESL) or English language learners (ELL) materials may see high circulation and, therefore, need frequent replacement. In general, you need to keep at least one current dictionary for Spanish, French, German, and whatever other languages are studied or spoken in your community. Putting them in the circulating collection makes more sense than letting them gather dust in the reference collection. This section should also have learning materials in foreign languages that reflect the interests and needs of your community.

Weeding in the 400s is really an opportunity to fine-tune your collection. It's likely that you may have a basic set of stock dictionaries, foreign-language materials, and ESL and ELL materials here. But do you know what your community currently needs? How long ago were most of those materials acquired? Have demographics in your area changed? Take this as an opportunity to purchase new materials as well as replacements for standards. Items receiving heavy use, such as Test of English as a Foreign Language (TOEFL) guides and ESL/ELL materials, should be replaced regularly with new copies and titles to maintain currency and freshness in the collection.

The 500s (Pure Sciences)

This is an area where new scientific discoveries, theories, and techniques can make an outdated collection useless. The 500s contain subjects in which information is quickly dated or even proven wrong (physics, astronomy, etc.), as well as subjects in which information is nearly timeless (mathematics), so keep a careful eye on publication dates in this section, and do your homework, if necessary. Pluto is not a planet, and there's technically no such thing as a Brontosaurus. How old are your books on the International Space Station? Or on Mars expeditions?

Do your best to keep up-to-date in this section. It will be a heck of a job, for sure, but consider pulling everything five years and older for examination. Basic historical works on science, such as Darwin's *On the Origin of Species,* should be retained, but weeding must be aggressive in the more time-sensitive areas to ensure the availability of accurate, up-to-date information. Let's take a look at the breakdown of this section:

507 / Science Experiments

Weed based on condition and use, and check for outdated materials or safety standards. Consider asking a local classroom teacher to come in and evaluate the section. His experience (particularly as one who assigns such experiments) can be invaluable when deciding what to keep or replace.

510 / Mathematics

Weed based on condition and use, but retain a collection of the basics—algebra, geometry, trigonometry, and calculus. Update with revised editions. In these times of Common Core, it's important to make sure the materials you have reflect what today's students are learning. As with the books on science experiments mentioned above, consider asking a local classroom teacher to come in and evaluate your collection for timeliness and completeness.

520 / Space and Astronomy

The field of space and astronomy changes rapidly, so keep on top of this section and weed on an annual basis when possible. Discard titles that include Pluto as a planet, books on old space missions, and titles that do not have an international balance. Stargazing books should be attractive and discuss relevant technology.

550 / Earth Sciences

Weed books that do not reflect current theories and science on geological activities. Replace books that have outdated information on major disasters—such as the eruption of Mount St. Helens and the 2005 earthquake in Pakistan—with more current books that examine the long-term aftermath. Field guides for amateur fossil and rock hunters can be kept as physical condition and circulation allows.

560 / Paleontology

It might not be obvious, but changes occur in this field as well. (Poor Brontosaurus.) Circulation should *not* be a factor in keeping outdated dinosaur books—the popularity of this topic with students may mean that even outdated books are checked out.

570 / Life Sciences

Weed and replace books on genetics, human biology, and evolution because of the rapid changes in scientific practices. Weed titles on ecology that appear dated—do you still have titles from the 1970s on the shelf? Update classics with newer editions, if possible. Keep an eye out for books that are sensational or political in tone.

580 / Botanical Sciences

Most of your botany books can stay, based on appearance. One thing to watch for would be field guides that promote edible or medicinal plants and herbs—ensure that they meet current safety guidelines.

CHAPTER 5

Shelf by Shelf: 600s

The sheer scope of the 600s is what makes it so daunting. You'll approach the medical books in a much different way than the cookbooks. Parenting books go in and out of style like you wouldn't believe, and how about those trusty (ahem, dusty) car-care books? And you will note that in several places throughout the 600s, there are very similar books in other Dewey areas. For a small library, it may make sense to combine those items and reclassify as needed.

The key here is to take each section piecemeal rather than worrying about them as a coherent group. It may even be best to break the task up among colleagues, if possible.

610 / Medicine and Health

Snap on your latex gloves, and get ready for surgery—it's about to get bloody. Be ruthless in weeding your health and medicine books. Leaving outdated information on your shelves in these areas is irresponsible (not to mention dangerous). Don't fall into the trap of "But if I don't leave this, we'll have nothing on this topic!"—that doesn't fly in the medical section. You do have access to the Internet, yes? And a knowledgeable librarian to guide patrons to appropriate medical information? You're looking at a one- to three-year copyright range for these books. Regularly weed books on rapidly changing and high-interest topics, such as AIDS, cancer, fertility, and pregnancy.

Books that focus on disabilities or major illnesses need to be scrutinized for outdated terminology and treatment options. As mentioned in other sections, this is the time to check against what you also have floating around in other areas of the collection. Titles by cancer survivors are often found in 362 as well as 616 (and possibly in with your biographies)—is that really helpful for your readers?

When it comes to classic titles in this section, most libraries need keep only the current year of *Physician's Desk Reference* and other drug directories, replacing with new editions as available. Reference works such as *Gray's Anatomy* should also be the most current edition, sending the previous edition to your circulating collection.

620 / Engineering, Auto Repair

Unless you are a special library, you likely do not have much in your 620s. If you have basic books on engineering, construction materials, or the like, weed based on usage and condition. You may also want to consider placing items in other areas of the collection for higher visibility, if possible. (Some engineering titles can also fit in 720 with your architecture books.) It may be helpful to weed your 620s and 690s at the same time to eliminate crossover books and reclassify some titles for ease of access.

This is also the area where you may have too much shelf space devoted to car-care books. So many libraries that I've helped weed have ditched those multiple shelves of car manuals, and no one complained. It is hard. Many years were spent acquiring those collections—and many dollars, as well. But unless people are actually using them, it's time for them to go. Replace with one of the car-care databases that are now available. Not only are they less expensive than the print materials but they are likely to get more use—it's easier to take printouts to your garage than to lug one of those diagnostic manuals, which are really meant for professionals anyway. *I hereby grant you permission to discard your old Chilton manuals if they are not in use (and I'm betting that they are not).*

630 / Agriculture, Gardening, Pets

If your library serves patrons in the farming or agriculture industry, keep specialty materials up-to-date with an eye on the newest techniques. If your patrons are more garden-variety (pun intended), then circulation is the main weeding criteria for this area. General gardening information does not age, but the materials themselves do, so keep an eye on worn and unattractive gardening books. No black-and-white illustrations here, please. Books that focus on organic gardening or the use of pesticides and chemicals should be reviewed for currency of information after three to five years.

When it comes to pet books, materials on various breeds don't go out of date, but your collection should reflect breeds that are of interest to your community, and the material should be attractive. Veterinary medicine and animal care are topics that do change, so keep those books no longer than a seven- to ten-year copyright span.

If hunting is popular in your area, use circulation records to weed out items that are no longer of interest and focus on what is popular for replenishment.

640 / Home and Family Management

This section can create hoarding issues for even the most passionate weeder. Who doesn't love a gloriously illustrated cookbook, even if all you can manage is a pot of spaghetti? Here is where your circulation reports will come in handy, giving you reasons to weed.

When it comes to looking for recipes, do your patrons actually use these books, or have they moved on to using the Internet for their recipe gathering (hello, Pinterest)? If your library is pressed for space, weed cookbooks that haven't circulated in the past two years. That may seem harsh, but the reality is that people no longer need a vast collection of cookbooks on hand to look up a recipe. Weed out books by celebrity chefs or that are based on popular diets once their popularity has waned. Replace classic cookbooks, such as *The Betty Crocker Cookbook* or the America's Test Kitchen series, with new editions when available. Larger collections can get away with keeping more unused titles on the shelf, as space allows, weeding with an eye toward three to four years last circulation date rather than two.

When it comes to sewing, weed books with outdated styles and illustrations. Same with home furnishings, and it bears noting that you may have the same type of books both here, at 645, and at 747.

On the surface, parenting books may seem to go out of style, but that's not the case. Although there are always trends and new theories, and parents insist on having the latest information, there are also classics, such as books from La Leche League and Dr. Spock's *Baby and Child Care*—and it's inexpensive to replace these with new editions as available. (Side note: I had a librarian tell me once that she didn't need to weed a 1987 edition of *The Womanly Art of Breastfeeding* because "you stick the baby on the boob and that's that! Who even needs a book about it?").

650 / Business and Management

This is another area where you may be tempted to keep basic books, but the reality is that your patrons will likely only want the latest advice and trends. Look at a five-year weeding cycle for these books. Books on résumés, job searches, and careers should be more in the three- to five-year range. Classics in the field can be kept longer based on condition. *Larger collections can keep basic books, if patron demand warrants and space is not an issue.*

670 / Manufacturing

Think about what you are collecting in this section. Do you have repair manuals for appliances? If so, are they actually used by your patrons? It's possible that some resources may contain information of historical value, but in the case of repair manuals, is that really very likely? Also, keep an eye out for older books on technology that may reside in this section.

690 / Building Construction and Home Repair

Keep materials current in this section, as codes and trends change often. As noted previously, it may be helpful to look at your 620s and 690s at the same time to weed out crossover books and reclassify some titles for ease of use; there are also architecture crossovers between the 690s and 720s.

CHAPTER 6

Shelf by Shelf: 700s

Weeding the 700s may not be as daunting as it seems. It's a huge number of shelves in most libraries, but the weeding decisions aren't very complicated. The key in this section is to have a good handle on what your community requires and what is actually being used. Sure, oversize art books are beautiful, but are they practical or cost-effective if there is no interest in them? How about your sports section? Do you have books on specific teams that no one in your area follows?

Oversize books and those with nonstandard bindings can pose a problem in the 700s. Many art books are large and weighty. The solution for some libraries is to house an oversize collection elsewhere in the library—but I would caution that you need clear signage and notes in your catalog, or those books will never see much use. You also need to decide if those items (which are usually quite expensive) are allowed to circulate or not. Many popular craft books are wire bound or plastic-spiral bound, which does not bode well for multiple checkouts. The best advice here is to make careful purchase decisions and to accept the fact that those particular items may need frequent replacement.

As noted in the installment on weeding the 600s, use this opportunity to re-catalog books that may be a better fit in other areas. Gardening books find their way into the landscaping section, engineering often gets into architecture, and home repair and remodeling mixes in with decorative arts. Exert local control, and work with your technical-services team to ensure that these materials are getting the best possible exposure to your patrons.

The following offers more specific tips for particular sections of interest.

709 / Art History

For the most part, general histories of art and music can be kept based on usage and condition. It's important to note, however, that age quickly becomes a factor here. If your most recent title on modern art is from the 1990s, it's time to update. Now is also the time to weed out black-and-white books.

712 / Landscape Architecture

As noted above, pull books here that seem better suited to 635 (Gardening).

720 / Architecture

Older books on the history of architecture are safe to keep as long as they have decent illustrations and are in good condition. Weed home-building books after ten years to ensure that code information is current. Pay attention to books of local interest (are there famous buildings in the area, or popular home styles of note?), and keep up on current trends.

This is another tricky cataloging area. Check right now—where in your library would you find a book on renovating a kitchen? Mistakenly here at 729, at 747 with interior decoration, or at 643 with housing and household equipment? Why make your patrons chase down similar books?

737 / Numismatics

Keep coin and stamp catalogs current, replacing books that provide market valuations and price guides after three to five years. Evaluate the usage these materials get in your library, and consider thinning the collection as necessary.

740 / Drawing

Keep basic books on techniques such as drawing, painting, and sculpture. Replace as needed with fresh and attractive new materials when possible. If you collect compilations of perennially popular comic strips (Calvin and Hobbes, Garfield, Peanuts), replace as they become worn if circulation warrants.

Consider reclassifying graphic novels of adult and YA-interest from 741.5 to a unique shelving classification that highlights them and assists patron discovery. Pull these titles and shelve them at the end of your fiction section, for example.

745–749 / Decorative Arts, Interior Decoration, Crafts, Antiques

There is an awful lot going on in this small Dewey range. In some libraries, you may find that more shelves are allocated to this four-number spread than to the rest of the entire section! This is likely to be a very popular section in most public libraries, so keeping it well organized and up-to-date is crucial.

Weed general interior-decorating books after five years. Keep a close eye on books based on television-shows or by celebrities—those may go sooner. As previously mentioned, check to see if you have similar books shelved elsewhere. Weed with an eye to appeal and trends—it's safe to say that you no longer need the twenty-five books showcasing Feng Shui home design that your library purchased in 2001. (And really, don't those belong in 133 anyway?)

Keep various craft books based on use, but be on the lookout for outdated colors, styles, and materials. Discard books on crafts and trends that are no longer popular in your area.

Feel free to keep books on antiques and collectibles—especially identification and price guides—until new editions are available for replacement. As with numismatics and stamp collecting, evaluate the usage these materials get in your library, and consider thinning the collection as necessary.

780 / Music

Make sure your collection is well rounded and includes basic works on a variety of musical styles (blues, classical, country, folk, jazz, opera, pop, rock, New Age, world). If your library collects sheet music, weed based on condition and use.

790 / Performing Arts

This section often includes celebrity biographies or memoirs by performers writing about their work. Consider moving these titles if you have a separate section of biography and memoir. Most titles here can be weeded based on interest and condition.

793 / Games and Sports

Books on professional sports teams can quickly become outdated, so weed and replace as needed. For general titles on games and sports, weed and replace as rules and trends change, and try to not keep much that's ten years out of copyright. Do watch for gender and racial bias in sports and athletics. Books on fishing and hunting can be kept for longer periods of time if condition warrants.

CHAPTER 7

Shelf by Shelf: 800s and Fiction

E ven though they are separate collections, I think it makes sense to look at weeding the 800s and the Fiction collection together, because much of the advice translates to both collections. Weeding the 800s isn't really that much of a challenge, mainly because the content of the books in this section tends to age well, and the materials are often in constant circulation to students. It becomes a personal point, however, because many librarians cry "Sacred!" when they think of literature. Based on your shelf space, you may be able to keep classic items longer. However, there are some specific sections to pay extra attention to.

In general, use the same guidelines that you would in any section: if it's tattered or hasn't circulated well, it's time to go. But what does "circulated well" mean in the 800s? This is where it's important to know the needs of your patrons. Students always need to reference literary criticism of the classics, so if something hasn't gone out in two to three years, find out why. Is that author no longer assigned? Are there newer, more interesting works on the author? Are teachers requiring a specific cutoff of copyright dates? I once helped a student gather all of our library's literary criticism on George Orwell, only to be told that she couldn't use most of our books because the teacher wanted citations no older than 2000. That was definitely one of those cases where the idea "oh, this particular material doesn't age" became a liability for the library. Make the effort to contact your local schools and community colleges for reading lists.

And much like the Chilton car manuals in the 600s—I give you permission to weed your set of *Best American Short Stories* if they do not circulate well. You'll be fine keeping only the last five years' worth.

811–812 / Poetry and Drama

Unless your library has a mandate to collect poetry or plays, most items should be weeded after five or six years of no circulation. Inspect your single-copy plays for damage such as highlighting or margin notes. Replace poetry anthologies with new editions—*The Princeton Encyclopedia of Poetry and Poetics,* for example, was updated in 2013.

817 / Humor and Satire

This is an area that tends to be trendy. Do you still have books by Jerry Seinfeld or Paul Reiser on the shelf? Have they been checked out recently?

822.3 / Shakespeare

Most small- to medium-sized libraries will be fine with keeping only one edition of the "complete works" while also collecting current paperback editions of the most popular plays. (Check with local schools to see what appears on reading lists.) Never underestimate the power of an attractive, fresh copy.

Fiction

Weeding the fiction collection usually gives even the most hardhearted librarian pause. After all, we're supposed to be the guardians of books, the keepers of the fiction flame, and that novel from the 1980s that hasn't gone out in fifteen years is surely someone's favorite book! Even though I'm a ruthless weeder, I'll admit that I'm thrilled that WorldCat shows me almost 500 libraries still own a copy of my favorite glitz-and-glamour novel from the 1990s, Beverly S. Martin's *Juffie Kane*.

It's very difficult to remain objective when it comes to fiction. What works stay depends on your shelf space, your readership, and the overall size of your collection, so there are a lot of variables. Naturally, you'll want to refer to your library's collection-development policy and mission as reminders and keep your community's demographics and interests in mind.

Some people find weeding fiction very easy, since they can just make their case off from circulation records or visible condition. Others find it incredibly difficult because there is not a set of stringent guidelines for fiction, as there are for nonfiction. So why can't we just keep our fiction, since it doesn't really "expire" the way that some nonfiction does?

Merle Jacob, former head of Collection Development for Chicago Public Library (and my weeding mentor), outlined the following important considerations for weeding fiction in her 2000 ALA program, "Weeding the Fiction Collection; or, Should I Dump Peyton Place?"[1]

> *Relevance:* Weeding fiction that is no longer being read creates a collection that is a better reflection of the community's needs and interests and encourages usage.
>
> *Currency:* Weeding ensures that the authors and titles in the fiction collection are up to date and of interest to your patrons.
>
> *Appeal:* Weeding worn and unattractive materials makes the collection physically appealing. Whether we like it or not, we live in a visual age. We compete with websites, television, movies, ads, and bookstores, so we need to look good.

Circulation: Weeding studies show that circulation increases after weeding because patrons can more easily browse less-crowded shelves.

Accessibility: Weeding makes it easier for patrons and library staff to find materials quickly.

Key Strategies for Weeding Fiction

These are general starting points, and different libraries will have different reasons for choosing a date range when it comes to pulling fiction off the shelves.

Use circulation records. As a starting point, if a fiction book has not circulated in the last three years, it should be considered a candidate for weeding. For some libraries, that time period may be shorter, depending upon the size of the collection. Other libraries may be able to stretch it out to five years, if space is not a consideration. A second set of numbers to look at, however, is the age of the book. Basic advice for fiction titles that are not considered classics or not written by a perennially popular author is to discard books that are older than ten years if circulation has waned.

Condition is the next point. Is the binding bad? Would you check this book out? (You can judge a book by its cover!) Condition is an easy place to start, but it's not as simple as just tossing the ugly copies—if that's your strategy, you will likely end up with some disgruntled patrons. Keep in mind that titles become worn out because people are reading them. On the flip side, if a book has been on the shelf for several years and is still in pristine condition, that tells you something, too. And never underestimate the power of replacements. Replacing a tattered or outdated-looking copy may boost circulation of that title—I've seen it happen over and over again.

So what do you do when you have a book that's in great condition and is on the edge of your selected time frame for weeding? Think about author name recognition—is this an author who is still writing? Still living? A book in a series, perhaps? An author who made a big debut but hasn't written anything for a long time or has seen a marked decline in popularity? Older single-title authors are usually prime targets for weeding. But, of course, everyone's definition of older will vary. Most of the time, ten years is a good benchmark. Smaller libraries with less space may need to use five years. Another category of prime weeds is the earlier or lesser works of authors who have died. This sounds mean, but let's face the music—they're not writing anymore, so if what you have on the shelf isn't going out, feel free to let it also rest in peace. Same goes for the minor titles of classic authors and more obscure classic titles that don't circulate.

It may be a good time to revisit the questions I posed in chapter 1:

- Would I be embarrassed if the library didn't own it?
- If I put this on display, would it go out?
- Does the book fit the needs of my community? Does it have local interest?
- Is the author still living and writing?

Classics and Old Favorites

One of the biggest issues that comes up when weeding fiction is the balance of classics and popular titles. It's useful to remember that everyone has a slightly different idea of what a classic is. Find a list you are happy with (*Great Books*, the *Modern Library 100 Best Novels* list, *Fiction Catalog*), and use it as a guideline for weeding items that aren't circulating well but might be good candidates to keep. Check with local schools for required or recommended reading lists. If staff members are crying foul over seeing their favorite authors headed for the chopping block, try a display of staff favorites to see if there is any interest.

Multiple Copies

Your library's collection development plan should address multiple copies—how many to purchase, when to purchase (hold ratios), and how many to keep. This is purely based on your budget and shelf space. Once interest in a title has waned, simply retain the number of copies specified in your plan. Most libraries will only have space for one, but larger collections may get away with three.

I've had great luck using AbeBooks (www.abebooks.com) and local used bookstores to obtain near-new hardcovers of older series titles. Local used bookstores can be a great source for old hardcovers in good condition, or look for a vendor online. In addition, don't discount mass-market paperbacks as replacements—you aren't going to find a nice hardcover of Grafton's *A Is for Alibi*, but it's OK to just keep purchasing mass markets to replace it.

Getting Over It

As noted in chapter 1, the response to "This is someone's favorite book!" is, "And we'd be happy to ILL it for him." Don't get me wrong—I do respect that weeding can be hard for librarians who hold every book near and dear to their hearts. And I have my favorite authors and titles as well. But libraries are not museums, and they do have very real space constraints. Popular fiction makes up the majority of circulation in most public libraries, and it's our job to maintain a useful, attractive, and interesting collection.

Special Considerations for Series

When it comes to series, if the author is still popular or still writing, it is important to keep series intact. Because most fiction series are sequential and best read in order, it is helpful to retain the complete run if the size of your collection permits. In addition, the release of a new title in a series may create interest in older titles. That said, if older series books haven't gone out in seven years or more, it's hard to imagine that even a new release will make them circulate, so feel free to weed—and weed the whole run. Which bring us to another point: if circulation stats show you could weed two or more books from a series, you need to either keep those two, or weed the entire run. Figure out what circulation numbers you are comfortable with, and then the decision should be made to either keep them all or get rid of them all—don't weed book five of a series just because that's the one that's gone out the least.

The more I write about or give programs on weeding, the more I've come to realize that sometimes it feels as though you need permission to weed, and someone to tell you that you've made the correct choice. It's easy enough to justify deselecting the computer books from the 1990s, the medical books that are seven years old, the dinosaur books that talk about the Brontosaurus, or the outdated travel books. It's a lot harder to think about possibly getting rid of someone's all-time favorite read. So I'm giving you permission to weed that fiction collection. Remember that libraries are not museums, and they do have very real space constraints. Popular fiction makes up the majority of circulation in most public libraries, and it's our job to maintain a useful, attractive, and interesting collection. A better selection of books—ones that are actually being used—should be every librarian's goal.

NOTE

1. Mary K. Chelton, "Weeding the Fiction Collection: Or Should I Dump Peyton Place?" *Reference & User Services Quarterly* 40, no. 3 (2001): 234-9.

CHAPTER 8

Shelf by Shelf: 900s and Biography

I f you're not too traumatized from weeding your fiction collection, then it's time to move on to the 900s. The special call-out sections of the 900s are travel and biography. Other portions of the 900s should be weeded based on condition, currency, and usage.

Books on current affairs should be weeded after three to five years; some titles may be retained for historical perspective as space allows. Most general history titles on various historical time periods can be retained if they are in good shape and are circulating, but do watch for dated material—please tell me you don't have books that refer to the Soviet Union in the present tense. This is also especially true for your geography and map sources.

910–919 / Geography, Travel

While physical geography doesn't shift quickly, boundaries certainly do. Weed with an eye for changes in political boundaries and country names.

For travel guides, weed after two years. Replace annually if the budget allows. An outdated travel guide is fairly useless to a traveler. Sure, people can check online, but the reason they came to your library to get that book was so that they didn't have to print out everything from the Web! I'll never forget the librarian who scoffed at me when I weeded *Fodor's New York City, 2000*—in 2004. "It's still useful, not that much changes in a big city like New York, all the tourist stuff is the same every year." I stared at her and simply said, "Twin Towers," as I discarded the book.

Core List of Travel Guidebooks

Naturally, libraries will have varied collections based on patron needs and requests, but keep in mind as you are weeding and replacing that most public libraries should have the following *current year* guidebooks available, at a minimum:

USA	Chicago
Hawaii	New York City
San Francisco/Bay Area	Boston
Los Angeles	New Orleans
Las Vegas	Florida Keys
Austin	International

Maintain country and regional guides to perennially popular travel destinations such as Italy, France, the United Kingdom, Israel, the Caribbean, Mexico, and Central America. Purchase guides to specific cities as needed.

It's also useful to add general guides or those about unusual destinations, such as the Lonely Planet or Rough Guide series; books on family or budget travel; guides to national and state parks; adventure travel; and Disney guidebooks. Be sure to follow the twice-annual Travel Roundup feature in the September 15 and April 1 issues of *Booklist* for guidance on replacement titles.

Biography

For most general biographies, anything that hasn't been checked out in three to five years is probably due for some inspection: Is the person no longer of interest? Are there more recent books out about the person? Biographies of popular figures and celebrities can be weeded once demand and popularity have receded, often in about a year. Benchmark titles of historical figures can be kept longer, if space allows.

If you're basing your weeding on copyright date, my rule of thumb is that for celebrity bios, think three (maybe squeaking to four, for an enduringly popular person) years from publication depending on your space issues. For historical bios, up to ten to fifteen years is reasonable, as long as the books are in use and are in good condition. And really, keep in mind that although a book on Lincoln (or whomever) published in 1992 might still be valuable and interesting, it's likely time to at least consider buying a newer copy of it. (Recall the anecdote from the section on the 800s, where a student couldn't use the literary criticism on Orwell because the teacher required a copyright of 2000 or newer.)

Also, think about how many different works you might have on one particular person. For an enduring historical figure, two or three is probably plenty (again, if you have the room), unless you know of a specific assignment where these books might all get checked out. Keep up with new releases on famous personalities—political and historical figures in particular.

940 / Europe

As noted earlier in this chapter, this is an area where you should keep a careful eye toward shifting boundaries. There have been, and continue to be, major changes in Europe, with countries experiencing political upheavals that have an effect on their borders and names. Cultural change is also rapid in much of Europe, and your outdated books reflect poorly on the collection. Reconsider any modern history of a country in Europe if it does not address current issues.

CHAPTER 9

Other Areas of the Collection

Weeding the Reference Collection

If reference sources are not being used in your library, they are just taking up space that could be repurposed. There is no magic number for how many items you should keep—in fact, the current trend we're seeing is that many libraries aren't keeping anything in reference sections anymore, and are simply moving titles into the general circulating collection. I encourage most small and medium public libraries to see if that is something that would work. It's useful in two ways: it gets those items into the hands of patrons who might actually use them, and it gives you something you can track, so you can see if the items really are (or are not) being used. If you have a title you are questioning, it makes a world of difference to be able to prove that something is or isn't being used. In a library where I worked, we decided to drop our reference shelving down about 80 percent. After weeding for condition and age, we moved the bulk of the "good" leftovers into the circulating collection. This freed up our space and then put those items either into the hands of our patrons . . . or on the next weeding report.

Reference can be tricky, since there is usually not a usage report available for reference items. As noted elsewhere in this book, attempts can also be made to track some reference usage, for example, by asking patrons to tick a piece of paper attached to the front of the book; or asking patrons to not re-shelve reference items. At the end of the day, a shelver can make note of items that have been used and left out.

At the very least, most libraries should feel free to discard older editions of standing reference titles. General encyclopedia sets and subject encyclopedias, if still purchased, do not need to be kept once a new edition is acquired. Almanacs, which used to be kept for ages, can also be discarded when the new version comes out. In this digital age, it is rare to have patrons who are using them for historic research.

Carol Singer's *Fundamentals of Managing Reference Collections* (see "Suggested Reading") offers an excellent template for a Reference Collection Development Policy, which is freely available online. www.alaeditions .org/web-extra-fundamentals-managing-reference-collections.

Weeding Media

Weeding audiobooks, DVDs, CDs, or any other non-book format is really not much different from weeding your print collection. Previous chapters can tell you what you really need to know—that you need to weed based on condition, usage, and what your goals are.

But there are a few considerations to keep in mind when looking at a media collection. Are you weeding because you have run out of space (a common problem in media collections, especially for audiobooks)? Then your main factor should be circulation. Choose a last-circulated date (two years is a good starting point for most media), and pull from there.

Format Matters

Who is your audience? Don't be so quick to pull your audios on cassette (I know, I know) if they are still in use—according to the *New York Times*, the last car to come equipped with a tape deck was manufactured in 2010. That's not too terribly long ago. That said, if the collection is not getting much use, it may be time to ditch them wholesale. Tapes are fragile, and it's quite likely that the bulk of your collection is in poor condition.

Even though most millennials or digital natives aren't even remotely interested in CDs, the majority of your audiobook patrons may still want them. Get to know who is using the collection, and what devices they use, before you make any decision to weed.

Downloadables are certainly the latest technology, but weeding a physical copy simply because the library has access to a digital one is not always appropriate.

Special Consideration for Audiobooks

As noted above, you can follow the basic weeding guidelines for your audiobooks, such as weeding outdated nonfiction topics and keeping series fiction intact. It may seem that there would not be any reason to keep a title in audio that you wouldn't keep in print—but there is an exception. The audio format has one extra layer that print does not—the narrator. Many listeners seek out the well-known readers (think Barbara Rosenblatt, George Guidall, and Jim Dale) and will listen to whatever they read, no matter the author or subject. Keep that in mind when weeding.

Special Consideration for DVDs and CDs

Look to your collection development plan for guidance on how to weed your DVD and CD collections. Are you maintaining a collection of popular materials exclusively? Are you collecting nonfiction films or documentaries to supplement your print materials? Weeding decisions should be made based on use, popularity, and wear, and you should pull television and feature film DVDs that have not circulated at least once during the past year. It's a safe bet that there is either something wrong with the disc or patrons have lost interest in the title. Space is the other factor here. If you have space, it's not hard to hang on to the slim cases of DVDs and CDs a bit longer.

VHS is a rapidly disappearing format, and most libraries should be clearing out this collection if it still exists. The format is simply too fragile and the mode of playback too inaccessible at this point.

It's tempting to sit back and say, "Well, the fragility of these formats means the collections are self-weeding!" Don't make that mistake. Use the same careful consideration you would use for your print collections, and let the "good stuff" in your media collections shine.

The Seattle Public Library has internal weeding guidelines for their CD collection, which are reprinted here with permission.

Weeding Magazines and Newspapers

In most public libraries, periodical subscriptions subsist of general interest titles meant for casual browsing and local interest titles. Most libraries recognize the transitory nature of paper periodicals, and no longer attempt to keep a full run of every magazine. A browsing collection can be difficult to assess, since most of the issues are read in-house and not checked out as frequently as other materials. But with budgets diminishing, cuts often need to be made, and care should be taken to keep subscriptions that get actual use. A simple way of tracking periodical usage is to attach a slip to the front cover of magazines, saying something along the lines of "DO YOU READ THIS MAGAZINE? We are currently conducting a usage survey for our magazine collection. If you enjoy reading this magazine in the library, please take a moment to make a check mark here. You can also always stop at the desk and let us know your preferences!"

Even when it is obvious which periodicals get regular use, it can be hard to decide how long of a run to keep. This decision can be purely based on space, but keep in mind that most general interest magazines are rarely used three to five years after publication date. Is it worth it to store them? It can also be helpful to check your holdings against what is available full-text in your library's databases.

In your collection development plan, address these four key points:

1. how to track patron usage and interest
2. how to display current issues
3. how long to keep back issues
4. where back issues will be stored and how patrons will access them

Seattle Public Library Weeding Guidelines for CDs

Weeding CDs

The goal for the system-wide CD collection is to provide broad coverage to serve our patrons who place holds and our patrons who browse. Due to limited space, individual branches are unable to provide deep CD collections that can respond to every request. Space for these collections is limited, so ongoing weeding is necessary for a collection to fit in its designated area. As this collection is also heavily used and subject to damage that can negatively affect the patron's enjoyment, worn and damaged materials need to be discarded to make room for new CDs arriving on a continual basis.

Weed for Condition

As with all collections, relying on Dusty Shelf reports for collection maintenance activity yields mixed results. The most practical way to proceed is to weed on the basis of condition. Systematically going through every disc and checking for scratches is the only sure way of capturing items that are not fit for circulation. Using a Dusty Shelf report slows this process down and misses items that should be withdrawn but are skipped because they are not on the report.

Weed for Age

Age is a secondary technique that can be used to identify "midlist" titles that were popular on release but have aged-out. Again, a Dusty Shelf report is not essential for identifying items in this category. Look for the physical barcode and label changes to quickly identify older items. For example, if you find any CDs with a green line above the barcode, those items were in your collection in 2003. Those may be excellent candidates to send to FOL, if you need to make space for newer materials. Anything with a barcode affixed to the back of a jewel case dates from Old Central. Any barcode (no matter where affixed) that begins with an alpha character (usually an A) is at least 10 years old. Publication dates are usually included on the CD itself or on the backside of the container or insert (usually in small print) but staff should understand that classic titles reissued (Michael Jackson or the Beatles as examples) would be of persistent interest, the press date notwithstanding. Packaging and barcode placement are very good guides: anything packaged in the black polyboxes or with the x-range film RFID tag affixed to the disc itself are the most recent additions to the collection.

Weed for Coverage

Think also about weeding for coverage. Maybe the local collection is too heavy on holiday music or there are too many folk/roots titles, etc. Staff could trim these sections down to a more usable representative sampling.

Do E-Books (and Databases) Need Weeding?

E-books and databases do need to be weeded, in the sense that they should not be left in place simply because they aren't taking up actual space. After all, patrons still have to search through outdated information to drill down to the "good stuff" if you just keep adding e-book titles and not removing any. Libraries should strive to have their electronic collections meet the same standards as the print collections. The process of making weeding decisions remains much the same for e-book copies as it does for print copies: evaluate the number of times the book was accessed, searched, or downloaded, as well as when the item was purchased (using records generated from the library catalog or the vendor).

In general, it's probably too soon to start looking at e-books as a replacement for print collections. E-books are a great way to supplement a print collection but I wouldn't actually let that influence my print purchasing, at least for now. There are still the same circulation issues as there are with print (one item, one checkout), but there are fewer people able to utilize the material—not everyone has an e-reader or is interested in e-books—so we're pretty far from the tipping point. However, it's a good idea to weed the e-book collection in conjunction with physical books. It may be useful to keep an e-book version of a classic or a formerly popular fiction title while weeding the physical copies, which will free shelf space for new titles.

In 2012, the CREW Manual added an addendum on e-books (www .tsl.texas.gov/sites/default/files/public/tslac/ld/ld/pubs/crew/crewe booksaddendum12.pdf). There is good advice there, including a lengthy discussion on how to think about weeding as part of overall ecollection development.

The issue is that, removing the links to items—or the items themselves—is not usually an easy process. Libraries often cannot do this themselves, and must ask vendors to do the actual removal—if they will. It becomes even harder when working in a consortium, which many libraries do for electronic collections. However, it may be possible to suppress records in your ILS, which can be helpful.

Databases

As budgets shrink, many libraries are realizing they need to take a close look at their databases. This can be an easy choice: patron use dictates keeping or discontinuing a database. A subscription database that does not show substantial use (considering the cost of the subscription) over a time period of a year should be removed or replaced. All database vendors should be capable of providing a library with usage statistics, although this can be tricky—one vendor may track number of clicks, another tracks time spent within the product, and yet another tracks the number of searches. Library staff should determine what statistic tells the best story of usage, and use that as a starting point. Consideration should also be tipped toward the coverage the product offers versus coverage available in print or elsewhere.

CHAPTER 10

Special Considerations for Youth Collections

While it is my belief that the weeding steps outlined in the shelf-by-shelf chapters translate to children's collections, there are some additional considerations. With a youth collection, whether in a school or public library, it may become habit to think, "Well, even an outdated book on X topic is better than no book at all." *Please* do not fall into this trap! Students deserve better than this—and their grade may depend on it. It's also easy to settle back on the "This was my favorite book when I was this age" school of thinking. If you are having trouble weeding a personal favorite, put it on display or try to hand-sell it (not aggressively—someone has to want to check it out to read it, not to get you off their back!).

Youth Nonfiction

Because most youth nonfiction titles will be used for school needs, it is *imperative* that these materials are kept up to date. Science and Geography in particular must be aggressively weeded. Young users are not as savvy as adults and will not be able to make the same judgment calls that an adult can when choosing material, and are therefore more susceptible to going right ahead and checking out that book on space exploration from 1989.

Youth and YA fiction

Popular interest trumps all here. If a book hasn't circulated in three years, it's not likely that it's going to be checked out any time soon.

Look at classics in terms of authors as much as books. I'm going to say it. Award winners are not sacred and should be withdrawn when they are not circulating. If in doubt, try to generate interest with an easy display of award winners. Replace those that do circulate with new, fresh copies as much as your budget allows.

Outdated covers are terrible across the board, but they are the kiss of death when it comes to youth and YA books. Check for updated paperback versions of seminal YA works in particular.

Much of your YA fiction is probably flavor-of-the-month, so make a point of clearing out the non-circulating items to make room for the new books.

Board Books and Picture Books

The very nature of board books makes them prime candidates for heavy weeding—they get chewed on, beat up, and can often be weeded on condition alone. Picture books are also well-loved, and usually come back with smudged or drawn-on pages. Replace what's popular or classic, and move on.

Youth Series Fiction

Multiple copies of series books often mean messy stacks. Determine what's still popular, and purchase replacements for worn or outdated versions.

Replace missing titles or sequels as necessary, but don't be afraid to weed an entire run if there are gaps that cannot be filled and interest has waned.

Sample Weeding Schedule for Children's Collections

As with the sample schedule detailed in chapter 1, these are generic guidelines meant to be adapted to any library's particular collection size and needs.

> *Biennially*: Board Books
> *Every three years*: Audiovisual
> *Every five years*: Picture Books, Early Readers, Fiction, Paperbacks, Series, Nonfiction, Biography, Parent/Teacher, Reference (These items should all be weeded on an ongoing basis by condition, but a full review should take place no less than every five years.)

Nonfiction Circulating Collection

If an individual title is no longer popular, the library should not retain more than one copy of it. With a few exceptions, the library should retain only the current edition of a title. Titles that have not circulated in two years are considered for weeding. Weeding cycle is every five years. There are a few sections that warrant special attention:

300 / Social Sciences

Common subjects include family issues, social issues, environmental issues, government, military, holidays, folktales and fairy tales. Youth Services maintains a large collection of folktales and fairy tales representing a wide range of cultural traditions, and this portion of the collection is usually not time sensitive.

400 / Language

Common subjects include English grammar, sign language, dictionaries, and foreign language instructional, as well as recreational reading material; these materials tend to age well. The collection should be evaluated every five years.

500 / Science

Common subjects include science experiments, natural sciences, dinosaurs, mathematics, pure sciences, biomes, botany, and animals. As these topics tend to be time-sensitive and change rapidly, this area of the collection should be evaluated every two years.

Board Books

We expect these books to be treated roughly; therefore this collection needs to be weeded biennially. Titles that have not circulated in one year are considered for weeding.

Fiction

Most fiction, including picture books, early readers, and series titles should be retained based on popularity with our current young patrons. Titles that have not circulated in two years are considered for weeding. Weeding cycle is every five years.

CHAPTER 11

Weeding Gone Wrong

U nfortunately, library weeding gets a bad reputation, thanks in part to weeding horror stories. In 2013 Highland Park (MI) High School was accused of throwing out a large collection of history materials, including some rare items, which had been cultivated over a fifty-year period. (Highland Park's emergency manager says the collection was thrown out by mistake.) Also in 2013, The Urbana (IL) Free Library discarded nearly 10,000 items, apparently just based on age, rather than condition or use. The discarding was done at the director's command—while the head of adult services was on vacation. (The now-former director stated that the ten years was only the report benchmark and that books were individually evaluated.) While it's hard to find anything good in this story, it should be noted that the library is undertaking a large-scale RFID project, and that is absolutely the time to undergo a massive weed. It's just a shame that it doesn't appear to be a carefully planned process. 2014 saw news stories from school libraries in Racine (WI) and Boston (MA). The media in Chattanooga, (TN) had a field day interviewing the former library director, who was more conservative about weeding, after the new director weeded almost half the collection over two years. Patrons in Albany County, California, formed their own protest group when they noticed that most of the shelves in their branch libraries were suddenly only half-full.

What usually happens is that a disgruntled (sometimes justifiably so) staff member sets off the alarm to the public about what's happening behind closed stacks. Or worse, a patron spies a Dumpster full of discarded material and immediately jumps to the conclusion that the library is enacting a modern-day book burning. Employees who do not feel their concerns are being heard or their professional opinions are being considered may decide they have no choice other than to become a whistle-blowers. Patrons who do not understand the selection or weeding process are understandably alarmed when they see a mass number of items removed from their local library.

It pains me to read about these "bad weeds" for a number of reasons. First and foremost, because I've been there—on the dark side. As I shared in the introduction, in 2001, while working for the Chicago Public Library, I was accused by a local politician of destroying books while working on a massive and much-needed weeding project at one of the regional branches. I was part of a team whose members were experienced in collections, and we had a plan to move, replace, and discard a large amount of material—but, unfortunately, that plan did not include communicating with the public to let them know what was going to happen. Nor did we do a very good job of communicating with the branch staff, who felt that they were being pushed aside by a group of outsiders. The experience really opened my eyes to the need for an open path of communication and the need for staff buy-in. Lucky for me, I have also worked on weeding projects that went very smoothly, even when working with high numbers of books.

I also hate to hear these bad weeding stories because they raise the hackles of patrons, taxpayers, and book lovers everywhere, and lead them to believe that weeding is never a good thing. Hearing such horror stories tends to bring on the knee-jerk reaction that no book should ever, ever be discarded, which simply isn't feasible. And, finally, these stories are painful because they illustrate that there are still plenty of librarians and administrators who do not understand the fundamentals of weeding.

Ideally, a library wouldn't need to perform such drastic weeding projects. If a collection is weeded on a regular basis, a section at a time, and maintained well with new materials, it rarely requires a large, hard-to-ignore weed. When a major project is needed, it should be planned out carefully, and communication is a key part of that planning. It's not particularly difficult to get the message out to your staff and patrons.

Communicating with Patrons

If a large weeding project is planned, the word should get out before the work commences. The director should make a statement on the library's website, in the library newsletter, or to the local press. Take command of the situation rather than let speculation or rumors take hold. The general reasons for weeding should be discussed, as should some details about how the project will work and impact patrons (i.e., patrons may notice empty ranges while the evaluation process is going on; patrons should expect to see replacements coming in X weeks, etc.). It's important for everyone to keep in mind that weeding isn't always about ridding the shelves—sometimes it's about getting fresh new copies of the exact same titles.

In the case of ongoing weeding, there doesn't need to be a formal announcement, but staff should be prepared to answer questions from curious patrons ("Why are half the Graphic Novels missing from the shelf?" "I'm sorry for the inconvenience! We've pulled that section and it's currently on a book cart in the workroom while we check how much use the books get and search for new ones to add to the collection. Is there something I can grab for you?")

In either case, staff should use positive terms instead of negatives when talking about weeding and should never complain to patrons about the bad materials that were on the shelf. (The Cart of Shame should be an inside joke, unless you need to use it to prove a point!) Instead, they can explain that the library is making room for new materials, making the shelves easier to navigate, and replacing outdated information with current information.

The way you dispose of discarded material will also have an impact on how the public reacts. (See page 10 for more detail on what to do with discards.) If the public knows that material is being reused or recycled, they may feel better about the weeding process overall. If materials need to be thrown in the trash, the library director needs to make a statement regarding the types of materials that are being thrown away (outdated medical, law, books in unsalvageable condition, etc. are good examples to use here), so that everyone is clear that "perfectly good books" aren't being destroyed.

The Milwaukee School of Engineering has a page on their website devoted to the topic of weeding at the library (www.msoe.edu/community/campus-life/library/page/2012/book-weeding). One of the best parts of this page is that it includes the following language:

WHAT IF YOU SEE A BOOK THAT YOU DO NOT FEEL SHOULD BE WEEDED?

Tell us! Stop by the library and talk with one of the librarians or send us an email!

Because of the many factors that are implicated in the decision to remove a book, each case is different. However, the library staff will seriously consider the wishes of all members of the MSOE faculty, staff, or student body who inform us that the book should remain in the library collection!

To repeat, no book will be permanently removed while it is a candidate for removal. Books will only be permanently removed after the MSOE Community has had a sufficient opportunity to comment on the lists of candidates for removal.

In addition, the page describes, in very simple terms, the general guidelines that staff use for weeding:

CRITERIA FOR SELECTING BOOK WEEDING CANDIDATES

In deciding whether or not a book is a candidate for weeding, the MSOE Library staff attempt to answer the following questions:

- Is the book's content outdated or largely outdated?
- What do members of the faculty say? Do members of the faculty recommend that the book be kept?
- What do members of the staff say? Do staff members recommend that the book be kept?
- What do students say? Do members of the student body recommend that the book be kept?
- How many times has the book circulated? Has it circulated within the last five years?
- Is the book irrelevant to the needs and interests of customers?
- Has the book been superseded by something else? Has a subsequent edition been added? Is there a better book that should be obtained instead?
- Is the book physically damaged and beyond repair?
- Can selected books be obtained easily and quickly through Interlibrary Loan?
- Is the book requested by other libraries via Interlibrary Loan?
- Is the book considered a "classic" contribution to the field (and therefore, it would be retained)?
- Is the book a second copy? Are there good reasons to retain multiple copies of a book? (e.g., class readings, etc.). Other questions may also be investigated.

Even better? The site offers links to PDFs of lists of weeded items. Talk about complete transparency—I'm in awe. Putting statements like that out to the public can really help patrons understand that weeding does not happen in a vacuum, and that it is a necessary task. Weeding is not a mechanical process. There is emotion involved, there is thought involved, and it takes the same amount of skill to build a collection as it does to cull one. Successful projects will include keeping the staff and the patrons informed to help avoid speculation and negative assumptions.

Tales from the Front

These stories come from a "Weeding Tips" article on Booklist Online, *published June 17, 2013 (www.booklistonline.com/Weeding-Tips-Tales-from-the -Front-Rebecca-Vnuk/pid=6240597).*

Everyone seems to have a weeding horror story, and several librarians have shared theirs with me. Read on, and see if you can relate—or feel a sense of relief that perhaps your weeding experience wasn't so bad!

> While working in a large academic library, I chose to weed the law books in the circulating collection. Over 75 percent were outdated, and they were discarded. We never had a single complaint about such a huge weed—it appeared that no one ever missed them!

> I happened to open a book one day and pulled out the date-due card. It looked heavily foxed, indicating it was ancient—only to find that the bottom of the card was pristine white. I decided to have a look at some more books and found the same issue. So I asked a long-term employee when the collection had last been weeded, and she said never. I went into my office and drafted a one-page set of weeding principles. I presented it to my city manager and explained that it was time to rotate the stock. He said OK, and we pulled a substantial chunk of the collection, including a mass of hopelessly outdated nonfiction.

> In my high-school library, we began the process of weeding books from the shelves that had collected years and years of dust from lack of use. Some of the books were dated to the early 1900s! As we began the process, we noticed some books looked chewed on. We just assumed that having been on the shelves for so long, they had deteriorated. However, one day, when we were working on the same shelf, from opposite ends, I removed a book from the shelf and in front of my eyes was this tiny little mouse. I am not sure if I was more frightened than it was—but I would say that I jumped a few feet in total

fear. The mouse took off in the opposite direction. My coworker took over the job for me.

When we moved into our new library, the city seemed content to finance only bricks and mortar. To wheedle city funds, I looked for evidence we needed new books. I found an armload of travel guides to countries that no longer existed (Ceylon, Rhodesia, Belgian Congo) and career books in which illustrations pictured only males in plum jobs. In my hunt, I passed a droopy unabridged dictionary on the reference desk. It was published four decades past. We didn't bother rebinding—it went to the trash.

I weeded the 800s last year and lost track of the number of volumes I pulled that were original to the building's construction in 1902. Tiny, tiny books that had been library bound, full of onionskin paper and those peculiar ownership stamps that look like punches. I'm not exaggerating when I say that out of the 50 percent of the existing items I weeded, fully half were more than 100 years old, full of insects and dry rot.

A few years ago, I weeded the 600s in a medium-size suburban library and pulled off a gem called *How to Raise Your Mongoloid Child*, copyright 1954. I regret to this very day that I didn't take a picture of if before I threw it out. *[Author's note: As mentioned in chapter 1, I have also discarded a similar book, sad to say.]*

When I was weeding a school-media collection, I decided that my criteria for nonfiction would be that if any book had a copyright older than my mother-in-law, it was going to be tossed—including the astronomy book that said, "One day, man will walk on the moon." Problem was, that left me with almost no books.

One of my very first projects was a massive purge at a remote storage facility. Imagine a block-wide building filled with books of every description, and running around the perimeter were high shelves packed with fiction from the late-nineteenth to the mid-twentieth century. A coworker and I quickly reduced that collection—on the fly, as it were—by at least 80 percent. It was a bloodbath. We were Huns. My own reading tastes are a little perverse when it comes to interesting old books, and I'm as likely to be reading that trendy best-seller from 1913 as the one from 2013, so this was a trial by fire. Our liberal-arts educations got quite a workout, and on the whole, I think we did a fairly good job. And, of course, much of the stuff we were getting rid of was precisely the kind of public-domain titles now glutting e-readers, something even I with my oh-so-space-age RocketBook didn't envision back then. But, still, sometimes I reflect on what an utterly satisfactory and highly original reading lifetime I could pass among a library comprised of just one day's weeding during that project.

Tech Services thought we had a good way to weed old editions of standing orders. When a new edition came out, we'd put in a slip that indicated the old edition should go to our department for withdrawal, carefully indicating the bar code of the edition to withdraw. The books would then be switched when being shelved. Well, we stopped that practice when we found the current edition had sometimes been sent back with the withdrawal slip in it. We're pretty positive a new edition of a very expensive reference book actually got withdrawn and recycled and another one was on the way to the recycling bin when it was caught and we were able to salvage it.

CHAPTER 12

The Importance of a Collection Development Plan

A collection development plan is something that every library needs, especially when it comes to weeding. Many librarians feel a sense of unease or uncertainty when they approach weeding. We all want reassurance that what we're discarding isn't something that will be needed. We want to know we've made the right decisions.

What helps with those decisions is a solid collection development plan or policy. (For all intents and purposes, the terms are interchangeable, although you may find a policy document is shorter than a full "plan.") Having a plan in place puts everyone on the same page and can save a lot of time and frustration at all stages of the weeding project. Although it can't tell you what individual titles to keep, it can give you firm guidelines of what should—and shouldn't—remain on your shelves.

What's Your Plan?

Does your library have a plan? Have you seen it? If the answer to either of those questions is anything but a resounding yes, then don't even think of starting a weeding project. Other questions to ask once you've laid eyes upon the document: Is your plan basic or comprehensive? Who had input? When was it updated last? I'm always surprised when I talk to people about weeding and discover that there is no plan in place, or the plan was last updated in 2004, or maybe there is a plan but only the department head has read it, or it's only consulted when there is a challenge to materials.

A collection development plan serves both an internal and an external purpose. It's the librarian's guide to what to buy and what to collect—as well as why and how to discard—and it informs the public about the principles upon which selection decisions are made. A written plan can also provide a basis for continuity over time and through personnel changes.

Putting weeding into your plan is a smart (and in my opinion, essential) idea. A collection development plan is meant to guide staff, and weeding is part of the collection development process. Having guidelines in writing gives staff something to refer to and something to point to when questions arise, and it serves as a defense against public questioning of the weeding process.

Creating (or Updating) a Plan

The Arizona State Library has a wonderful comprehensive training document on the elements of a collection development plan, and rather than reinvent the wheel, I encourage everyone to read their guidelines (http:// apps.azlibrary.gov/cdt/weeding.aspx). There are also many books on collection development that address creating plans, including Vicki L. Gregory's *Collection Development and Management for 21st Century Library Collections: An Introduction* (2011); Peggy Johnson's *Fundamentals of Collection Development and Management* (2014); Holly Hibner and Mary Kelly's *Making a Collection Count: A Holistic Approach to Library Collection Management* (2011); and Carole Singer's *Fundamentals of Managing Reference Collections* (2012). ALA also offers a "Workbook for Selection Policy Writing," which includes a sample template, at www.ala.org/bbooks/

challengedmaterials/preparation/workbook-selection-policy-writing. (Details on all of these can be found in the "Suggested Reading" section at the end of this book.)

In addition, a simple web search will bring up dozens, if not hundreds, of plans. Find the documents of similar institutions, and see what appeals to you as you structure your own.

Your plan can be anything from a few pages to a long document. My advice is to craft general statements about the collection as a whole, citing goals and objectives and outlining responsibilities. I would then suggest taking the time to list every section individually, with the relevant purchasing and deselection information. The size and scope of your library will dictate how long or detailed your plan needs to be, but I think every library will benefit from pulling out each selection area. You don't need to necessarily outline the weeding procedure in this document (which may be better kept in an in-house guideline document).

For an example of this, see the Glen Ellyn (IL) Public Library's "Collection Development Policies, Procedures, and Plan" (www.gepl.org/about/policies/collection-development-policy and reprinted in the appendix). I worked on the original version of this document in 2008, when I was head of Adult Services at GPL. Notice how there are all three terms used in the name—*policy, procedure,* and *plan?* It clearly lays out every section of materials selection and briefly describes the goals of collecting in each Dewey area. There are separate sections for various formats as well as a separate Youth policy.

Once your plan is complete and approved by your board, make sure it makes the rounds. Every staff member should have a print copy or a link to the internal copy, and a copy should either be posted in a public place in the library or kept at the reference desk. If possible, post the document on your website—not only for your public but for the use of your fellow librarians.

And review and revise as needed. Every three to four years is probably sufficient, and the revision can likely be knocked out in a single committee meeting.

Using your Plan for Weeding

If you've written your plan by section, the plan should make it clear when sections should be evaluated, what publication dates should be used when making decisions, and what exceptions should be made. For example, the sample plan (page 17) plan lays out that the Dewey 300s should be evaluated every other year to see if weeding is necessary. It goes on to state

> Tax guides are kept for 7 years. Multiple copies are weeded after the current tax year. The college guides and test preparation books are kept up-to date by standing-order plans. Titles in the legal, personal investment, colleges guide, and test preparation areas need to be evaluated every two years and will be considered for weeding if they have not circulated in three years. All other areas should be weeded every 5 years. Titles with the exceptions noted above will be considered for weeding if they have not circulated for 5 years.

That's pretty clear advice. And, really, clear advice is what helps ease the uncertainty of weeding.

Be sure to check the collection development plans in the appendix. I've handpicked a selection of really good, clear plans from a variety of library types and sizes, all of which can offer guidance and make excellent starting points.

Annotated Sample Collection Development Plans

These plans have been collected as prime examples of effective weeding guidelines. Many of the following documents are freely available online at the time of this book's publication, and URLs have been given.

All excerpts have been reprinted with permission.

Morton Grove Public Library (IL)

Collection Development and Materials Selection Policy

(Former, 1992–2005)

The full document is available online at www3.webrary.org/inside/coll devtoc.html.

THE MORTON GROVE PUBLIC LIBRARY (MGPL) serves a population of 23,270 (2010 Census) with a collection of approximately 125,000 volumes. While their board has now approved a new, shorter collection development policy, the Library was known for the comprehensive plan that was available online for many years (many libraries took advantage of this and used the MGPL plan as a starting point). Written in 1992 and updated on a regular basis until 2005, the library is currently using a shorter, more easily updated board-approved document with much more general terms. The original document is currently available online for archival purposes at www3.webrary.org/inside/colldevtoc.html, and a small portion of it is reprinted here.

While it is a very long document, I think it is perhaps the finest example of a comprehensive and complete overview of the collection, and it is a superlative guide for staff. What is most notable is the fact that each section of the collection gets a paragraph on "Retention and Weeding" and a "Development Plan." For example:

Religion (200–299)

The religion collection is an overview of topics of interest to the general public, including such topics as theology; concepts of God; good and evil;

immortality and evolution; biblical studies; Christian theology, history, and doctrine; moral and devotional literature; and titles on comparative religion and religions other than Christianity. At present, the collection is strongly Christian and Jewish in content.

INFLUENCING FACTORS A significant influx of East and South Asian immigrants indicates the need to build collections oriented to Buddhist, Islamic and Hindu traditions. The prominence of an author in the area of Christian moral theology is of prime importance in the selection of materials from reviews in the standard sources. Christianity and its response to socioeconomic phenomena and problems are of constant interest to religious readers. Media reporting of current events can have a strong influence on selection.

280–289

A strong influence is the denominational representation in Morton Grove: Roman Catholic, United Church of Christ, Wisconsin Synod Lutheran, and Jehovah's Witnesses. Another factor is patron interest, regardless of denominational affiliation or lack thereof. For example, there is a continuing interest in the Mormon faith. There is a similar interest in cults.

290–299

Morton Grove has a substantial but declining Jewish population. The Library has collected virtually anything well-reviewed on Judaism and the Jews as an ethnic group. In recent years, there has been an influx of immigration from East Asia and South Asia to Morton Grove. The newly established Muslim school donated a basic collection of books on Islam. A few titles on religion in Korea were obtained with funds from a state grant.

SELECTION PLAN Using *Reader's Advisor* and *Books in Print*, the Library should augment its present collections in Buddhism, Islam and Hinduism with materials of interest to lay readers and relevant to current social issues. Attention should also be given to religious best seller lists, such as those found in *Publishers Weekly*. All religions and denominations are represented as fairly as possible, but sectarian materials of a proselytizing nature may be excluded in favor of unbiased, informative presentations.

290–299

The Library should focus on selection of titles on Islam, Hinduism, Buddhism and the other religions of South and East Asia—Jainism, Sikhism, Taoism, and Confucianism; perhaps titles on the faiths, as practiced in the countries of interest, i.e., Islam in India and Buddhism in Korea, could be acquired if patron interest should so indicate.

RETENTION AND WEEDING Condition of the book determines to a great extent its retention. The 200s are a more stable area with regard to retention and weeding than are many other areas. Classic works, histories and sacred texts of major religions, and important commentaries are retained. Books in poor condition and titles of an ephemeral nature must be withdrawn on annual cycle to maintain space for newer titles.

DEVELOPMENT PLAN Some modest retrospective buying is needed to represent the traditions of immigrant residents and to fill noticeable gaps, i.e., biographies of prominent church founders; however, the collection should remain fairly stable in size.

290–299

Concentration should be on popularly written or layperson-accessible titles of potential interest to practitioners of non-Christian faiths and to interested other parties.

Arts and Recreation (700–799)

The 700s encompass a wide range of subject matter of interest to students, casual art lovers, collectors, and handicraft and sports enthusiasts. The largest sections cover a wide range of arts and crafts, television and motion pictures, and sports. Virtually all items are at a popular level, with little scholarly material.

INFLUENCING FACTORS Patron interest and demand heavily influences purchasing patterns in arts and recreation. Current libretti for each Lyric Opera season, books on Chicago sports teams, and other recreational and informational topics of general public interest are essential purchases.

SELECTION PLAN Standard library selection sources are consulted along with specialty magazines in various fields such as *Opera News*, *Sports Illustrated* and *Petersen's Photographic*. Specialized publishers' catalogs such as Abrams, Watson-Guptill and Schirmer Books, and catalogs from sources such as the Metropolitan Opera and the Metropolitan Art Museum are also consulted. Opera libretti are ordered directly from Lyric Opera of Chicago. Most price guides for collectibles are added to the circulating collection rather than the reference collection. General guides should be treated as reference titles, while the more specialized titles are better utilized in the circulating collection.

RETENTION AND WEEDING Books on museums, sculpture or art history should be retained as long as use indicates continuing patron interest and demand. Information in these subject areas is stable and not time-dateable; however care should be taken to maintain currency and freshness in the collection by the regular acquisition of carefully selected new titles. The same applies to books on the history of movies, radio, theater, television and background information on various sports. Handicrafts, hobbies, collectibles and sports rule books should be kept current. Usage figures, condition, and currency of information should continue to be the standard criteria in the weeding process.

DEVELOPMENT PLAN The emphasis should be on keeping the popular topics (as noted above) current to fulfill patron expectations and needs. Photography should be developed, as funds permit, particularly in how-to titles and in collections of individual photographers. Purchasing in the fine arts should be influenced by patron demand and general public interest.

Applied Sciences (600–699)

The applied science and technology section serves an extremely wide range of needs: medical information, from personal health to disease coping and recovery; all aspects of home economics and management, including cookbooks, gardening, home and appliance maintenance and repair; electronics and engineering, including automobile maintenance and repair; management, ranging from starting and running a home business through improving one's management style and moving up the corporate ladder; manufacturing and building trades.

INFLUENCING FACTORS Public library patrons historically have extensive interests in areas such as business, personal health, cookery, do-it-yourself-projects, etc. Consequently, the demand for relevant, current information on these high profile subjects is always high.

SELECTION PLAN In addition to the standard selection tools, Science Books and Films and publishers' catalogs are used for selection. The standard sources generally provide adequate coverage of medicine, agriculture, home economics and management, while a greater reliance on additional sources may be necessary for other subjects such as electronics, engineering, manufacturing and building. Rarely should more than one copy of a title be purchased.

610–619

With the exception of classic works in such general areas as anatomy, nursing and first aid, most selections in the medical sciences should be aimed at the general consumer. It is important to cover as wide a range of diseases and treatments as possible.

620–629, 660–699

Engineering, Manufacturing, Building: Coverage of the more popular subjects in these areas needs to be broad in terms of level, from beginner to professional. Other subjects, especially some in the 660s, 670s and 680s, are too specialized and technical for a public library this size, in which case only popular works aimed at the non-professional are appropriate. Broad coverage is especially important in car repair books in terms of both year and model.

RETENTION AND WEEDING Weeding is based on the normal criteria of age, condition and usage, with the additional criteria listed below for certain subjects.

610–619

In general, medical books should be aggressively weeded to ensure that all sources are accurate and up-to-date. This is especially true for books on specific diseases. In other areas, such as dieting, smoking cessation, etc., weeding should be based more on usage level. While it is necessary to select a wide range of books in such areas, their popularity often drops quickly after a year or two.

620–629

In all areas, retention should be based on usage level and accuracy of information. In electronics repair, consideration should also be given to the popularity of the device; for example, there is little need to maintain anything more than a very basic collection on repairing black-and-white televisions.

Car Repair Books: Chilton's and Mitchell's multi-year or all-model books should be retained permanently (or as long as their condition permits). Single-model books should be retained as long as the model is popular, or a minimum of 5 years.

640–649

Regular weeding has left the collection in good shape. However, many new titles are added on a regular basis, so weeding must be done on a yearly basis to avoid overcrowding. Withdrawal considerations should be based on the condition of the book, excess material in any given area, or outdated information.

660–699

Manufacturing, Building: Until these sections are built up, and since information on these subjects is not quickly outdated, weeding should be fairly light so that the collection covers as broad a range of topics as possible.

DEVELOPMENT PLAN Overall, the 600s are at an appropriate level. However, within the manufacturing and building subjects that are appropriate for the library, increased purchasing is necessary to expand both the size of the collection and the range of technical levels (beginner to professional).

Geography and History (900–999)

The history and travel collection consists of popular works intended for a general audience, and supplemental material to support student use (mainly in United States and Western European history). Morton Grove patrons are great travelers, thus placing a considerable demand on current travel guides to most international and national locales. There are also numerous titles covering World War II.

INFLUENCING FACTORS Morton Grove is an ethnically diverse community, thus reflecting a wide range of subject areas that need to be addressed by the collection. The population demands current as well as classic works in the study of all aspects of history. Age and affluence create demand for all types of travel materials. Growth of the Asian population in Morton Grove will necessitate a further enhancement of the Asian history and travel collections.

SELECTION PLAN In addition to the standard selection tools, university press publishers' catalogs, *New York Times Book Review*, and *American Historical Review* are checked regularly. Generally, one copy is ordered unless strong patron demand is anticipated. Travel materials are selected through the standard tools as well as through publisher's catalogs such as

Hunter, Lonely Planet, Fodor, Globe Pequot Press, and Rand McNally. MGPL has standing orders for many annual travel guide series such as *Fodor's, Fieldings, Frommers, Mobil*, etc. Generally, one copy is purchased so that the library will have a wide spectrum of the world represented, but titles which are very popular, such as the *Mobil* guides, are often purchased in multiple copies.

RETENTION AND WEEDING Many works of history are classic titles and should be retained, such as the WPA guides to the states. Careful selection and anticipated demand also aid in determining retention. Titles on popular history are weeded as demand decreases. Travel materials are generally retained from 3 to 4 years, except for travel/adventure memoirs which are retained as long as circulation statistics indicate an interest in them. Multiple copies, materials in poor condition, and superseded titles are weeded on a continuing basis. *Public Library Catalog, Books in Print*, and *Reader's Advisor* may be consulted before withdrawing titles in this collection.

DEVELOPMENT PLAN This collection needs some attention in order to broaden coverage on areas of the world outside of Western Europe and the United States. Areas that need to be expanded include the Middle East, Asia, and Africa. Current thought should be represented along with classic texts and treatments. It is important to replace worn or missing titles in the heavy circulating area of travel materials. It is also important to keep in touch with the changing needs of the community and to monitor the demand for specific titles and subject areas.

Fiction

Classics of literature, popular best sellers, critically-acclaimed first time authors, and genre fiction (spy novels, gothics, romances, historical fiction, westerns) make up the fiction collection. Mysteries and science fiction, which includes fantasy, are separate collections for the browsing/ reading convenience of Library patrons. The primary purpose of the fiction collection is to satisfy the heavy demand from recreational readers for popular, new titles. Current best sellers are bought in multiple copies to satisfy anticipated demand. Emphasis is on American and English authors. Classic and popular current authors from other countries are included in English translation, but on a limited basis.

INFLUENCING FACTORS Fiction circulates well in the Library's community. In addition to recreational reading, the needs of student populations in high schools, numerous community colleges, universities, and continuing education programs for returning older students influence selection of authors and titles. Numerous adult book discussion groups in Morton Grove and neighboring communities create demand for critically acclaimed writers, classic authors, and noted foreign authors. A ready audience and a heavy demand for popular authors dictate selection in the best-seller category. Short stories generally appeal to a small audience; the selection of such titles should be restricted to major authors or award-winning titles.

SELECTION PLAN In addition to standard selection tools, book sections from the Chicago newspapers, and patron demand heavily influence selection. Popular best sellers are obtained in multiple copies to fill patron reserves on a one book to five reserve basis. Generally, only one copy is purchased of other titles, depending on demand. Clues for determining the number of copies to order include how many copies are being printed, the promotional budget, author tours, and selection by book clubs or guilds. Titles are ordered as far ahead of publication as possible, often without the benefit of a review, knowing that there is a heavy demand for major authors.

RETENTION AND WEEDING Literary classics, regional authors, and well-recognized contemporary authors are retained, sometimes in duplicate, as fits demand. Weeding of duplicate copies, books in poor condition, and of ephemeral authors must be done on an annual basis to maintain space for new books. Best sellers wear out rapidly because of high demand; they are either repaired, replaced, or withdrawn depending upon circulation, significance and current popularity of the author, and/ or availability. Donations frequently are used to replace worn, damaged best sellers.

DEVELOPMENT PLAN Very little retrospective development is needed, except for filling out the complete works of important and/or popular authors. An emphasis should be placed on replacing worn out editions of older, but important titles with new hardbound editions or new trade paperbacks so as to encourage patron use. New translations of classics that receive critical acclaim should be considered for purchase, or new editions purchased as needed to replace older versions that are worn, bound in library binding, or otherwise unappealing for patron use. The focus should be in having enough multiple copies of high demand books to satisfy patron requests as quickly as possible while maintaining collection depth by purchasing as broadly as possible.

La Grange Public Library (IL)
Collection Development Plan (January 2012)

The full document is available online at www.lagrangelibrary.org/lagrange/ documents/collectiondevelopmentplan2012.pdf.

THE VILLAGE OF LA GRANGE has a population of 15,550 people (2010 census) and the library serves a fairly affluent community. Their plan document states

> As a public library, our overall goal is to offer a collection that provides general support for the interests of our community. We participate in a consortium of eighty nearby public, academic, and special libraries, which provides our patrons easy access to over seven million items. Therefore, our local collection is focused on meeting the needs of the La Grange community. We primarily support the recreational and informational needs of our patrons. In fiction, this means a high-interest collection from a variety of genres, with broad coverage where interest demands. In nonfiction, we provide general information on a wide variety of subjects, with higher emphasis placed on topics of local interest.
>
> Our secondary objective is to provide educational support to students in local public, private, and parochial schools. Because our area schools have well-supported school libraries, we do not act in lieu of the school library, but we do work with the schools to provide some homework support materials to supplement the local school collections.

Their plan is broken out by Dewey area, and each area includes details on how often a section should be weeded, along with general criteria. It is notable that the plan utilizes numerical formulas showing the average age of materials and usage of specific collection areas. It is also incredibly thorough, covering each section of the collection by item type, in great detail.

The Adult Collection sections are shown here.

Adult Nonfiction
000 Computer Science, Information and General Works

DESCRIPTION
- This section includes books on computer instruction, the history of print and broadcast journalism, biographies of journalists and broadcasters, trivia, and UFOs and other unexplained phenomena.
- The collection is for a general adult audience, as well as for high school students.

PHILOSOPHY
In this section, we intend to keep a current and wide-ranging collection of computer instruction books, from patrons learning basic computer skills, to those needing more advanced application programs.

SELECTION
- The most recent editions of computer instruction books are purchased to keep the collection current.
- Books by popular broadcasters and journalists are purchased.

WEEDING
- Computer instruction books are weeded whenever a new edition becomes available.
- For other areas of this section, if a book has not circulated in 5 years, it becomes a candidate for withdrawal.

GOALS

- Circulation statistics and turnover favor maintaining the overall size of the collection.

STATISTICS

Relative Use	Active Use	Average Age	Turnover
1.04	56%	7	1.7

100 Philosophy and Psychology

DESCRIPTION

- This section covers popular psychology, paranormal psychology, and philosophy.
- The collection is for a general adult audience, as well as for high school students.

PHILOSOPHY

In this section, we intend to keep a current collection of books that give people guidance on how to effectively cope with grief, stress, anxiety, and other interpersonal issues.

SELECTION

- We purchase books by popular authors in the self-help area of psychology, because these authors may have popular television or radio programs, so they normally have many fans who will also read their books.
- Paranormal psychology includes books on astrology, ghosts, witchcraft, and dream interpretations, so it needs to stay current with the latest available information.
- Philosophy books need to take into account both Eastern and Western theories, from ancient times right on through to the present.

WEEDING

- Books in the self-help area of psychology should not be kept for more than 5 years, because new books are constantly being published in this area with new information, and new approaches to solving problems.
- Paranormal psychology books older than 5 years need to be weeded, unless we own classics in the field that need to be retained. Such titles can be replaced with reprints if older copies are badly worn or damaged.
- Classic works of philosophy should always be present in the collection, and only be replaced with reprints, if they are in poor condition.

GOALS

- Circulation statistics and turnover favor maintaining the overall size of the collection.

STATISTICS

Relative Use	Active Use	Average Age	Turnover
1.09	61%	8.8	2.0

200 Religion

DESCRIPTION

The religion collection refers to all books with religion as the focus. The collection is for a general adult audience as well as high school students.

PHILOSOPHY

In this section, we focus on Christianity, as the majority of the La Grange population identify themselves as Christian. We also attempt to keep myth and religious origin books on all major religions and regions of the world. The eastern religion books have also proven to be quite popular, particularly those written by or about the Dalai Lama.

SELECTION
- High circulating subjects include Greek mythology and the history of Christianity.
- The major world religions of Christianity, Judaism, Buddhism, Islam, Hinduism and Taoism should be well-represented.

WEEDING
- Weed religious titles after ten years, or three years without circulating.
- Retain classic titles on the history of major world religions, and books written by religious leaders.

GOALS
- Based on the 2010 circulation report, this collection should remain at its current size.

STATISTICS

Relative Use	Active Use	Average Age	Turnover
0.94	58%	8	1.6

300–329 Social Sciences

DESCRIPTION
This section includes books on sociology, statistics and political science.

PHILOSOPHY
In this section, we focus on popular titles in social issues and political science, and local and national statistics.

SELECTION
- *Sociology (300–310)*—Personal memoirs in this area are popular. The highest circulating subjects are adolescence, sexuality (including marriage and divorce), and cultural studies on African-

Americans and women. Cultural studies from the Chicago area, especially civil rights, are popular.

- *Statistics (310-319)*—This collection is minimal and only includes updates to basic information. Include books on Illinois and national statistics, such as circulating almanacs.
- *Political Science (320-329)*—Best sellers in this area are popular. Be aware of staying even with left, right, Republican, and Democratic viewpoints; also look for well-reviewed books so the facts in the "party" books are accurate.

WEEDING

- *Sociology (300-310)*—Weed these titles after five years, or two years without circulating.
- *Statistics (310-319)*—Retain only the most current local and national statistics, and replace with a superseded edition when available, such as a new census.
- *Political Science (320-329)*—Weed political science titles after five years, or three years without circulating. Retain classic titles on the Constitution and political history. Review existing titles for outdated information, such as regional name changes.

GOALS

- As more data become available online, re-assess the need to retain print titles in statistics.

STATISTICS

Relative Use	Active Use	Average Age	Turnover
0.72	42%	7.8	1.3

330–359 Economics, Finance, Law, and Military Biographies

DESCRIPTION

- This section covers economic history, personal finance, real estate, legal self-help, and military biographies.
- The collection is for a general adult audience, as well as high school students.

PHILOSOPHY

In this section, we intend on keeping a current collection on practical and sound investment philosophies by both popular and well-respected authors. It is also important to have legal self-help books by experts within specific fields of law. Biographies and memoirs of well-known generals and military officers give insight into battle preparation and the bravery and sacrifices made by soldiers within their units.

SELECTION

- Books on economic crises and corporate histories are popular.
- The latest books with new strategies on building personal wealth are sought out.
- Legal self-help books must keep up with changes in laws.
- Memoirs and biographies of popular military officials are purchased.

WEEDING

- Books in this section are weeded if they have not circulated in the last 5 years. Exceptions to this include books that are deemed "classics" in their field. Such books are replaced if there is an updated edition, or the particular copy on shelf is very worn or has physical damage to it.
- Books with new information that is more comprehensive and accurate on topics in this section will replace older titles that are lacking in accuracy, comprehensiveness, and new information.

GOALS

- Circulation statistics and turnover favor maintaining the overall size of this collection.

STATISTICS

Relative Use	Active Use	Average Age	Turnover
0.81	52%	7.0	1.5

360–389 Crime, Education and Commerce

DESCRIPTION

This section consists of titles on social services, criminology, education, commerce, communication and transportation.

PHILOSOPHY

In this section, we focus on current social issues, including crime. The education section and transportation section are limited to titles of local interest.

SELECTION

- *Social Problems and Services (360-369, excluding 364)*—Books geared toward students doing reports on social issues need to be kept very current.
- *True Crime (364)*—This is an area of extremely high interest, particularly gangsters and any crime in the Chicago area.
- *Education (370)*—Textbooks are extremely popular. We usually keep the two most recent editions of books published annually. Books concerning public education and how to get scholarships/ into college are also popular.
- *Commerce, Communications, and Transportation (380-389)*—Only well-reviewed titles are added due to lack of interest. Railroads and train transportation is very popular, especially any title related to Chicago railways. Guides to stamp values are also extremely popular and should be kept very current.

WEEDING

- *True Crime (364)*—Retain historical studies of true crime, especially in the Chicago area.
- *Education (370)*—Weed titles after ten years, or three years without circulating. Replace test guides with the superseded edition when available.

GOALS

- Based on the 2010 circulation report, this collection should remain at its current size.

STATISTICS

Relative Use	Active Use	Average Age	Turnover
0.94	52%	7.6	1.7

390–399 Customs, Etiquette and Folklore

DESCRIPTION

This section includes books on historical and ethnic costumes, tattoos and tattooing, American holidays, and urban folklore. Etiquette books, particularly business etiquette books involving practices in other countries and cultures, as well as titles on wedding planning are also in this section.

PHILOSOPHY

This collection contains popular works intended for a general audience. Books about costumes, fashion history, and standard works of folklore don't date as quickly as books on business etiquette and wedding planning. Holiday-specific books may only circulate once or twice a year.

SELECTION

- Emphasis should be on keeping the collection current and relevant to the interest and needs of the community.

- Be aware that materials date rapidly in business etiquette and wedding planning, so updated editions should be purchased rather than adding replacement copies.

WEEDING
- Condition, usage statistics, and currency of information should be taken into consideration; however, seasonal items may only circulate once a year.

GOALS
- Based on the 2010 circulation report, this collection should be re-assessed for weeding, as relative use is low.

STATISTICS

Relative Use	Active Use	Average Age	Turnover
0.85	57%	7.9	1.6

400 Language

DESCRIPTION
This section includes titles on learning languages, the philosophy and theory of languages, and dictionaries and translations. The collection is for a general adult audience.

PHILOSOPHY
In this section, we focus on modern European languages. All major languages should have some representation.

SELECTION
- Learning a language and English/foreign language dictionaries are popular (especially Spanish, French, German, and Polish). Narratives about word and cliché origins are also well used.
- Items on grammar and linguistics are not as popular.

WEEDING

- Language titles should be discarded after ten years, or three years without circulating.
- Replace dictionaries for modern European languages when a new edition is available.

GOALS

- Based on the 2010 circulation statistics, this collection should remain at its current size. We should expand the selection of workbooks for adults who are learning to read.

STATISTICS

Relative Use	Active Use	Average Age	Turnover
1.00	62%	6.7	1.3

500–549 General Science, Math, Astronomy, Physics, Chemistry

DESCRIPTION

This core collection covers the history of science, mathematics, astronomy, physics, and chemistry.

PHILOSOPHY

In this section, the Library intends to keep a core collection of books relating to the history of science, the various disciplines of mathematics, and current books on astronomy, physics, and chemistry. As new discoveries are constant in astronomy, physics, and chemistry, only up-to-date books should be retained. Biographies of researchers in these disciplines should be retained for student projects.

SELECTION

- Preference is given to starred reviews. Other titles should be strongly considered as there are few titles for the general reader published in these disciplines.

- Donations of recent (three years old or less) textbooks should be highly encouraged for all of the areas within this section.

WEEDING

- General science and the history of science should be weeded using circulation statistics.
- A core collection in the various disciplines of mathematics should be retained. Look for newer replacements for titles that are five years old or older.
- Currency is very important in the fields of astronomy, physics, and chemistry. Books that are five years old, or older, should be considered for weeding. If there is no replacement title, check the content of the book and make sure that the information is still up-to-date and meets current theories in the field.
- Textbooks three years old, or older, should be considered for weeding.

GOALS

- This section should maintain its size as a core collection.
- If relative usage in this section increases then secondary (non-starred reviews, more narrowly focused or esoteric titles) titles can be considered for the areas of greater patron interest.

STATISTICS

Relative Use	Active Use	Average Age	Turnover
0.87	54%	7.4	1.6

550–599 Earth Science, Paleontology, Biology, Botany, Zoology

DESCRIPTION

This core collection covers the natural sciences dealing with the Earth, its history and biology, and its plants and animals.

PHILOSOPHY

In this section, the Library intends to keep a core collection of books relating to natural history. As new discoveries are constant in paleontology and biology, only up-to-date books should be retained. Older books dealing with the species and natural history of plants and animals are often still useful, but should be reviewed every few years. Biographies of researchers in these disciplines should be retained for student projects.

SELECTION

- Preference is given to starred reviews. Books about animals are popular in this community.
- Donations of recent (three years old or less) textbooks should be highly encouraged for all of the areas within this section.

WEEDING

- A core collection in all of the areas should be retained. Field guides are an integral part of the core collection, but look for newer replacements for titles that are five years old or older.
- Currency is very important in the fields of paleontology and biology. Books that are five years old, or older, should be considered for weeding. If there is no replacement title, check the content of the book and make sure that the information is still up-to-date and meets current theories in the field.
- Textbooks three years old, or older, should be considered for weeding.

GOALS

- This section should maintain its size as a core collection.
- If relative usage in this section increases, then secondary titles (non-starred reviews, more narrowly focused or esoteric titles) can be considered for areas of greater patron interest.

STATISTICS

Relative Use	Active Use	Average Age	Turnover
0.59	43%	8	1.2

600-619 Technology, Medicine and Health

DESCRIPTION

This collection includes all aspects of medical and health information including human anatomy and physiology; diseases and treatments; nutrition, diet, and exercise; women's health and pregnancy; and childhood diseases and syndromes. Test books with practice exams for nursing students at all levels are also in this section.

PHILOSOPHY

Because this collection is primarily for lay people, families, and caregivers, most selections are aimed at the general consumer. Emphasis should be on keeping the collection current and relevant to the interest and needs of the community. The popularity of specific diets often drops quickly, so diet books should be replaced frequently.

SELECTION

- Currency, accuracy, and readability of materials should be considered along with a balance of alternative and traditional treatments.
- Materials date rapidly in medicine and health, so updated titles should be purchased rather than adding replacement copies.
- Anatomy and physiology guides should be heavily illustrated in color.

WEEDING

- Aggressive weeding should be done on an ongoing basis, as dated medical information can be dangerous.
- Primary consideration should be in keeping the collection current.

GOALS

- Based on the 2010 circulation report, this collection should remain at its current size.

- Books in medicine and health will always be in demand as the percentage of Baby Boomers increases.

620–629 Wiring, Small Engines, and Vehicles

DESCRIPTION
This collection includes books on electronics and electronic fundamentals, popular information on wiring, and small engine repair. This section also includes *Rules of the Road* manuals.

PHILOSOPHY
In electronics repair, consideration should be given to the popularity of the device. Car repair books are no longer purchased since patrons have access to the Chilton Auto Repair database.

SELECTION
- Select books with clear, color photographs, and precise, easy-to-follow instructions.
- *Rules of the Road* manuals in English, Spanish, and Polish should be updated annually.

WEEDING
- Primary consideration is keeping the collection current.
- Car repair books (particularly Chilton) should be weeded since patrons have access to the Chilton Auto Repair database.

GOALS
- Based on the 2010 circulation report, this collection should remain at its current size.

STATISTICS

Relative Use	Active Use	Average Age	Turnover
1.16	59%	7	1.8

630 Agriculture, Gardening, Pets

DESCRIPTION
- This section covers agriculture and its related technologies, including horticulture and animal husbandry.
- This is a heavily-used area with both core titles and more ephemeral (trendy or fashionable pets and gardening techniques) titles.

PHILOSOPHY
In this section, the Library intends to keep a core collection of books relating to general agricultural topics. It encompasses two areas popular with La Grange patrons—gardening and pets—and should be kept current with trends in horticultural techniques, species and types of garden plants, and species and breeds of pets.

SELECTION
- The La Grange Garden Club is a very active community group, so keeping a broad collection in all branches of horticulture is recommended.
- Refer to the American Kennel Club's list of top breeds to help in selecting breed-specific dog books.

WEEDING
- A core collection of general gardening books should be retained. Update older editions of classic works, where possible, and look for newer replacements if a title goes out of print.
- An attempt should be made to retain books about specific species and families of plants.
- Books on dog training should cover the different approaches to training and not just focus on currently popular authors.
- An attempt should be made to retain at least one book each about the less common, smaller pet species.

GOALS

- This section should maintain its size as relative use is equal to 1.00.

STATISTICS

Relative Use	Active Use	Average Age	Turnover
0.99	57%	8.2	2.2

640–649 Household Management

DESCRIPTION

This collection consists of general and specialized cookbooks including ethnic, seasonal, holiday, and diet-based titles, as well as books by popular chefs. This section also includes books on kitchen and bathroom remodeling. Sewing, fashion and beauty, and titles on starting a food-related business are also in this call number area.

PHILOSOPHY

This collection is aimed at the general reader and consumer. All types of cookbooks are popular and circulate frequently. Books on kitchen and bathroom remodeling are aimed at DIYs.

SELECTION

- Patron interest and demand influence purchasing as tastes, decorating styles, and fashion constantly evolve.
- Books on kitchen and bathroom remodeling should be highly readable with clear directions and color photographs.
- The J/Parent-Teacher Section in Youth Services serves the parenting/childcare community, so collecting for the 649 section has decreased.

WEEDING

- Since new cookbooks are added on a regular basis, aggressive weeding should be done to avoid overcrowding.
- Styles date quickly both in fashion and grooming.

GOALS

- Based on the 2010 circulation report, more titles should be purchased.

STATISTICS

Relative Use	Active Use	Average Age	Turnover
1.49	72%	7.3	2.3

650–699 Job Hunting, Starting a Small Business, and Home Improvement

DESCRIPTION

- This section includes books on job hunting, starting a small business, management, marketing, advertising, and do-it-yourself home improvements.
- The collection is for a general adult audience, as well as high school students.

PHILOSOPHY

In this section, the Library intends on keeping a current and updated collection of job hunting books, starting a small business, and do-it-yourself home improvements. These would include new editions of resume writing books, books on home-based businesses, and the latest methods and techniques in home improvement.

SELECTION

- Books that include the latest information on online job searching, social networks, and posting resumes and cover letters electronically are important to add to the collection.
- Finding books on starting a home-based business, that may include forming your own website to do business online, is something to consider.

- Magazines on home improvement and woodworking may have reviews of the latest books that incorporate the newest materials and techniques.

WEEDING

- Books in this section are weeded if they have not circulated in the last 5 years, and damaged books are withdrawn or replaced with a new copy of the same edition or replaced with a newer edition, if one is available.
- Older editions of books in this area are replaced with newer editions, as soon as they become available.

GOALS

- Based on factors such as relative use, active use, and turnover, this section should maintain its overall size in these subjects.

STATISTICS

Relative Use	Active Use	Average Age	Turnover
1.03	62%	7.6	1.8

700–730 Art History, Landscape Art, Architecture

DESCRIPTION

This section covers general books about art and art history, civic and landscape art (including landscaping as a profession), and architecture.

PHILOSOPHY

In this section, the Library intends to keep a core collection of books relating to general topics about art, landscaping, and architecture. Due to the La Grange Historic District and La Grange's proximity to the large number of Frank Lloyd Wright homes in Oak Park, books on architecture are popular with our patrons.

SELECTION

- Books on historic architecture (particularly Victorian) and restoration of older houses are especially in demand.

WEEDING

- A core collection of general books about art history should be retained. Update older editions of classic works, where possible, and look for newer replacements if a title goes out of print.
- An attempt should be made to retain books about specific styles of architecture.
- Books about Frank Lloyd Wright should be retained unless space considerations merit weeding.

GOALS

- This section should maintain its size as a core collection.

STATISTICS

Relative Use	Active Use	Average Age	Turnover
0.77	54%	9.2	1.9

740–779 Graphic and Decorative Arts

DESCRIPTION

This collection consists of instruction guides on drawing and painting, craft how-to books, titles on interior design and home decorating, painters and paintings, and photography.

PHILOSOPHY

This collection contains popular works aimed at the nonprofessional and hobby enthusiast. Information on collectibles and traditional antiques is still of interest, but price guides have decreased in popularity due to easy access of information on the Internet. Knitting still continues to be very popular. Information concerning art and artists is stable and not time-dateable. Since books in the fine and decorative arts tend to be expensive, consumers rely heavily on the Library's collection.

SELECTION
- Books on painters and painting should be illustrated in color and have good quality graphics.
- Select craft how-to books with clear, color photographs, and easy-to-follow instructions.
- Instruction books in photography should reflect the rapid changes in technology.

WEEDING
- Art books that are worn or have torn-out pages should be weeded or replaced.
- Craft books tend to be in paperback, so condition is a strong factor when weeding.

GOALS
- Based on the 2010 circulation report, this collection should remain at its current size.

STATISTICS

Relative Use	Active Use	Average Age	Turnover
1.16	63%	7.9	2.1

780–799 Music, Film, Television, and Sports Entertainment

DESCRIPTION
- This section includes biographies of popular singers and musicians, as well as books on the history of popular and classical music. It also includes biographies of popular and influential actors and directors, as well as books on the history of film and television. Besides this, there are also biographies of popular athletes from different sports, as well as sports histories.

- The collection is for a general adult audience, as well as for high school students.

PHILOSOPHY

In this section, we intend on keeping a collection of biographies of recent popular and critically acclaimed singers and musicians, as well as ones from earlier eras. Biographies of popular and critically acclaimed actors and directors that are currently working in film and television, as well as actors and directors from the golden years of film and television are also acquired. This section should also have a solid collection of sports biographies of current, popular athletes, as well as famous athletes from earlier times.

SELECTION

- We purchase well-written and comprehensive biographies of singers, musicians, actors, and directors that are current or from the past, and have a sizable body of work.
- We also purchase well-written sports biographies, and memoirs of popular athletes. Biographies of star players from local, professional teams are given top consideration, as well as local, professional sports team histories.

WEEDING

- Books in this section are weeded if they have not circulated in the last five years. Exceptions to this include books that are deemed to be "classics" in their field. Such books are replaced if there is an updated edition, or the particular copy on shelf is very worn or has physical damage to it.
- Baseball card price guides need to be current, as do books on sports teams that emphasize current player rosters.

GOALS

- Circulation statistics and turnover favor maintaining the overall size of this collection.

STATISTICS

Relative Use	Active Use	Average Age	Turnover
0.74	48%	8.5	1.6

800–829 Literature in English

DESCRIPTION

This section includes books on the craft of writing; American literature including poetry, drama, and essay collections as well as criticism and biographies of authors; and similar works by and about British, Canadian, and Australian authors in English.

PHILOSOPHY

In the Literature section, we keep a variety of titles on writing craft, including updated style manuals. Collections of works by important authors in the English language are kept as a core collection, along with biographies of the authors and works of criticism when appropriate. The addition of electronic databases with critical information has reduced the need for much criticism in print for educational purposes. Most well-reviewed, popular works on Shakespeare are purchased due to perennial class assignments.

SELECTION

- Books for this area are selected primarily by using professional review journals, paying particular attention to starred reviews and to works on popular authors and those who are studied in local schools.
- Biographies of authors, memoirs, and works by humorists often appear on best seller lists, and are usually purchased due to patron demand.

WEEDING

- Books in poor condition are weeded and may be replaced based on popularity.

- As "collected works" of important authors, particularly poets, become available, smaller individual titles may be weeded as superseded.

GOALS

Based on the relative and active use statistics, this collection is larger than current popularity requires. Careful weeding is appropriate to move the collection closer to ideal size.

STATISTICS

Relative Use	Active Use	Average Age	Turnover
0.46	32%	10	1.2

830–899 Foreign Language Literature

DESCRIPTION

This collection consists of plays, poetry, and literary criticism written by and about foreign language authors, and popular fiction and nonfiction written in Spanish and Polish.

PHILOSOPHY

Because the collection caters to the general public and accommodates high school students, the focus is on French, Italian, and Russian writers as well as the Greek and Latin classics. This section also includes popular fiction and nonfiction written in Spanish and Polish as there are many La Grange residents who speak these languages.

SELECTION

- Use *Public Library Catalog* to identify the classics in Latin and early Greek literature, and for selection of French, Italian, and Russian writers.
- Replacement copies or revised editions should be purchased to replace old or worn material.

- Select bestsellers and popular fiction and nonfiction for the Spanish and Polish circulating collections.

WEEDING

- While classic titles should be retained, attention should be given to books that are in damaged or worn condition.
- Circulation statistics are an important consideration as well as availability at other libraries.

GOALS

- Based on the 2010 circulation report, this collection should be aggressively weeded.

STATISTICS

Relative Use	Active Use	Average Age	Turnover
0.67	44%	8.7	1.1

900–919 Geography and Travel

DESCRIPTION

- This section consists of works on general world history, explorers, pirates, shipwrecks, and worldwide travel. It also contains atlases.
- There is some overlap with areas of ancient history and with books on current life in foreign countries.

PHILOSOPHY

The Geography and Travel section includes materials for students and "armchair travelers" as well as vacationers. We try to cover the entire globe with a mix of current guidebooks and narrative titles. Books on the other subjects in the section are purchased as interest warrants, with an emphasis on well-reviewed titles.

SELECTION

Our patrons travel extensively, and a wide variety of travel materials are necessary to meet their needs. In addition, there is great demand for very recent information. A number of standard "brand name" guidebooks (e.g., *Fodor's* and *Eyewitness* guides) are purchased for most areas of the world and supplemented by other titles as needed, with accuracy and currency of information guiding selection. These are updated as often as budget and publication schedule permit. The most popular travel locations receive closer focus, with standing orders aiding ready availability of perennially popular books:

- Florida
- Chicago and environs; Illinois
- Europe, especially Great Britain, France and Germany
- Loss of materials in this area requires frequent replacement.

Atlases are mainly housed with Oversized Books and in the atlas case in the Reference Collection. Books in the other categories are selected as popularity dictates (pirates, the Titanic, Great Lakes shipwrecks).

WEEDING

- This section is weeded regularly as new editions of guidebooks are purchased. With few exceptions, older editions are removed to allow for a wider variety of titles in the allotted space.
- Narrative travel books and guidebooks with an emphasis on history and culture are weeded less frequently, with circulation statistics and available space being most important. This also holds true for books on general world history and other subjects in this section.

GOALS

- This area is slightly smaller than desired according to the 2010 circulation report. Budget funds should be allotted to allow for frequency of updating this collection.

STATISTICS

Relative Use	Active Use	Average Age	Turnover
1.14	57%	7.6	1.8

920–969 World History

DESCRIPTION

This collection consists of ancient history, the histories of Europe, Asia, and Africa, World Wars I and II, and popular biographies on royalty, especially those of England, France, and Russia.

PHILOSOPHY

Popular works intended for a general audience and materials to support student use form the core of the collection. The ancient history section emphasizes the Egyptian, Roman, and Greek empires. Current conflicts as well as past wars involving the United States are also popular, in particular World Wars I and II, Vietnam, Iraq, and Afghanistan.

SELECTION

- Books about the rapidly evolving events in the Middle East as well as ongoing changes and developments in Africa are currently popular.
- Select titles written by significant authors to ensure books contain historically accurate information.

WEEDING

- Weed books that are damaged, worn, or contain information that is biased or historically inaccurate.
- Materials can date rapidly due to changes in governments, shifts in geographic boundaries, breakup of countries (i.e., the former Soviet Union and Yugoslavia).

GOALS
- Based on the 2010 circulation report, this collection should remain at its current size.

STATISTICS

Relative Use	Active Use	Average Age	Turnover
0.95	57%	7.5	1.7

970–999 U.S. History, Latin American History, and Pacific Island History

DESCRIPTION
- This section covers U.S. history, including state and local histories, as well as histories of Native American tribes.
- Also included in this area are histories of Latin America and the Pacific Islands.
- The collection is for a general adult audience, as well as for high school students.

PHILOSOPHY
In this section, we intend on having a broad range of books that includes presidential biographies and memoirs, histories of notable events, Native American tribes, and state and local histories.

SELECTION
- We purchase well-written and comprehensive biographies of U.S. presidents and other key political leaders, as well as biographies of notable historic figures in Latin American history.
- Books on U.S. presidential elections and significant events in U.S. history, such as the American Revolution and specific battles of the U.S. Civil War by notable historians, are given prime consideration.
- Any books on La Grange history are important to have, as well as well-written histories of Chicago and Illinois.

WEEDING

- Books in these areas are weeded if there are too many books on a specific U.S. president, so we tend to keep the newer ones. If the biography is a classic, we will keep it or replace it with a reprint.
- New historical research on the original 13 colonies, American Revolution, and Civil War will replace titles with older, dated information.

GOALS

- Circulation statistics and turnover favor maintaining the overall size of this collection.

STATISTICS

Relative Use	Active Use	Average Age	Turnover
0.84	54%	8.8	1.7

Reference

DESCRIPTION

- The reference collection includes both print and online resources, whose primary purpose is to supplement the educational and informational needs of the community. It covers all subject areas. We also have a selection of professional titles that assist with staff work, such as a collection of *Reader's Advisor* sources.
- Due to space considerations, much of the print collection is housed behind the desk as Ready Reference. A portion of it is also housed with circulating genealogy titles in the nonfiction shelves; much of the genealogy collection was donated by the local DAR chapter. The intended audience of the adult Reference collection is teens through adults, though it supplements the Youth Services collection as well.
- Online resources such as databases and eBook collections are available both in the Library and from the home computers of La

Grange cardholders. These subscriptions meet the needs of our residents "24/7" and also ease crowded shelves when they can replace print titles. The availability of full-text journal articles online is especially important to our collection since our periodical collection is of a more popular nature and of limited use in research.

- A small collection of local and Chicago history titles is maintained.

PHILOSOPHY

The Reference collection is used by students of all ages, members of the business community, and residents looking for current information on topics such as medicine and investment. Reference is changing, and some materials formerly owned in print have been superseded by online resources.

SELECTION

- We have standing orders for a number of popular Reference titles. Others are updated when availability and funds allow, in order to keep the collection as current and relevant as possible. New print titles are carefully considered for accuracy, usability by a general adult reader, and need, with perennial school assignments being an important factor.
- Selection tools include standard professional journals and catalogs. We also learn about new titles from publisher's representatives and at workshops and conventions.
- We subscribe to online resources both individually and as members of consortia in order to provide a wide variety of materials in digital format.

WEEDING

- The Reference collection is in constant flux. Weeding occurs regularly as new titles are added, both to maintain shelving space and to provide currency. Older editions are weeded when updates are purchased, or when the importance of timeliness dictates.

GOALS

- The Reference collection is gradually changing. Although fewer print titles are being purchased as more quality information is available online through database subscriptions, many patrons still prefer to use print sources, and local school assignments require a mix of print and digital sources. We will continue to monitor the collection and our patrons to determine when print materials have outlived their usefulness. We must also promote the availability of our online resources to increase their use.

STATISTICS

Relative Use	Active Use	Average Age	Turnover
N/A	N/A	9.2	N/A

Fiction

DESCRIPTION

- This collection is comprised of general adult fiction titles, primarily in hardcover or trade paperback format. Mass market paperbacks and graphic novels are shelved as separate collections.
- This collection includes genre fiction (mystery, science fiction, romance, horror, westerns) as well as popular and literary fiction. All books in this section are filed by the author's last name; genre titles are interfiled but receive a spine genre sticker.

PHILOSOPHY

La Grange is a well-educated community of readers who are interested in all genres of old and new fiction. Due to limited space, supply does not meet demand, particularly of current bestsellers. We try to meet demand by purchasing multiple copies of popular titles based on numbers of patron holds; duplicate copies are weeded when demand wanes to retain space for a core collection of classic and "back stock" titles. Because we focus heavily on *Reader's Advisor*, a deep collection is highly desirable to meet our patrons' needs.

SELECTION

- Books for this area are selected primarily by reading reviews in professional journals, as well as newspapers and popular and genre-focused magazines such as *Entertainment Weekly* and *Romantic Times*.
- Duplicate copies of popular titles are selected based on holds placed by our patrons.
- Special effort is made to purchase titles to maintain series.
- Formerly, our mass market paperback collection was composed solely of donations. We began purchasing them to allow collection of titles, especially romance and science fiction genre titles, which are published only in the mass market format. Replacements of hard-cover books may also be made in mass market paper. Donations of titles by popular authors may be added to the mass market collection, especially if they do not duplicate hard cover titles in our collection.

WEEDING

- Series titles that are out of print in hardcover or trade paperback may be replaced in mass market paperback to maintain complete series.
- Duplicate copies of popular titles are weeded as demand falls.

GOALS

- The relative use statistics show that this is a very high circulating area. We will need to find creative ways to keep up with demand, such as considering a rental collection.
- A broad and deep collection of fiction (with an emphasis on American fiction) is crucial to meeting the needs of La Grange patrons.

STATISTICS

Relative Use	Active Use	Average Age	Turnover
5.07	62%	8	3.3

Mystery Fiction

DESCRIPTION

This collection consists of works of mysteries and police procedurals. It does not include thrillers or other crime fiction where no "mystery" exists. Story collections by one author are kept in this section; those by multiple authors are in Literature 800–829. The collection is interfiled on the shelves with fiction, but has genre spine labels for ease of browsing.

PHILOSOPHY

We purchase a wide variety of mysteries, including both stand-alone and series titles. Popular series are retained as space allows, but individual series titles may be purchased by patron request or to introduce patrons to new authors.

SELECTION

- Due to the popularity of this area, most starred or well-reviewed debut titles (series or stand-alone) are purchased.
- Special effort is made to purchase titles to maintain series.

WEEDING

- As this area circulates well, much weeding is done by attrition as copies wear out or are declared missing.
- Popular, still circulating titles may be replaced with used copies, or purchased for the mass-market paperback collection if in print.
- Titles that do not circulate are weeded at three to five years, as space requires.

GOALS

- Mysteries are a high-circulating area; demand far outstretches supply. Selectors must be aware of currently popular subgenres, and keep up with trends like hybrid mysteries (mysteries crossed with other genre such as paranormal or futuristic stories), while continuing to purchase perennially popular types like British procedurals and historical mysteries.

STATISTICS

Relative Use	Active Use	Average Age	Turnover
1.75	68%	8.8	3.4

Science Fiction

DESCRIPTION

This collection consists of speculative fiction, marked with a "science fiction" spine label and interfiled with the fiction collection as a whole.

PHILOSOPHY

Science fiction is a well-recognized genre within the larger fiction collection and so is treated as a separate collection. It includes such popular subgenres as fantasy, alternate history, urban fantasy, and "hard" science fiction, but does not include horror.

SELECTION

- Books are located for this section by reading reviews in professional journals, supplemented by popular culture magazines such as *Entertainment Weekly.*
- Many science fiction authors write books in series. The selector should pay particular attention to keeping up with popular series (as judged by circulation statistics).
- Due to the small budget in this section, books in the *Star Trek, Star Wars, Doctor Who,* and other popular movie- and TV-based series have not been collected.

WEEDING

- A small core collection of titles important to the genre (such as *Dune,* the *Foundation Trilogy,* and *Ringworld*) should be retained.
- Circulation statistics will be the main criteria for weeding this collection.

GOALS

- While this is the least popular area of the fiction collection, the circulation statistics indicate that there is patron interest in science fiction. This section should maintain its size as a representative collection.

STATISTICS

Relative Use	Active Use	Average Age	Turnover
0.64	53%	8	1.6

Large Type

DESCRIPTION

The collection consists of fiction and nonfiction books in large type format.

PHILOSOPHY

The collection is primarily popular titles to accommodate the interests of the readers.

SELECTION

- Review bestseller lists in large print and non-large print, patron requests and books advertised in the media (former Oprah selections).
- Keep current with the Big Read and other local and national group selections.
- Select basic reference titles on computer skills, diet and nutrition.
- Select books with current medical information regarding vision impairment.

WEEDING
- In fiction and nonfiction, weed items that haven't circulated in 3 years.

GOALS
- The goal is to grow this collection to meet recent increasing demand for large print books.

STATISTICS

Relative Use	Active Use	Average Age	Turnover
1.6	73%	6.4	2.5

Graphic Novels

DESCRIPTION
This collection consists of two sections of graphic novels: fiction, shelved by author or series title; and nonfiction, shelved by Dewey Decimal number.

PHILOSOPHY
The graphic novel collection was developed in 2001 as a deep collection covering all aspects of publishing in this format. Examples from every era and every genre have been added to the collection, with the intention of providing examples of the full range of storytelling in the graphic format. The fiction section includes popular superhero titles, Japanese manga series, other series, stand-alone literary titles, etc. The nonfiction section includes any nonfiction titles written in the graphic format.

SELECTION
- Books are located for this section by reading reviews in professional journals, including the *Comics Buyer's Guide*.
- The selector should establish a relationship with local comics stores (such as Chimera's Comics in La Grange). This is an excellent way to determine local buying, and therefore reading, patterns.

- The selector should also join GNLIB, the graphic novel librarians' listserv. This is highly recommended as a source for general information and specific collection advice.

WEEDING

- Damaged titles will be considered for repair or replacement if warranted by their circulation statistics.
- In the future, circulation statistics will be the main criteria for weeding this collection.

GOALS

- The Graphic Novel collection is still growing and shows extremely high demand by all statistical counting methods.
- In the future new formats, such as web comics, will be considered for purchase.

STATISTICS

Relative Use	Active Use	Average Age	Turnover
1.94	77%	4.8	2.3

Audiobooks

DESCRIPTION

- This collection is primarily comprised of fiction and nonfiction titles on compact disc. Language instruction titles are also included, including English for foreign-born patrons.
- A steadily circulating collection of audiobooks on cassette still exists, but is no longer being maintained since the format is becoming obsolete.

PHILOSOPHY

La Grange has many commuters who listen to books while driving. In addition, titles are popular with travelers, seniors, and others in the community. We maintain a high-use collection of titles by popular authors as well as standards and classics.

SELECTION

- Selection is primarily done on a title-by-title basis, but may include standing orders.
- Titles are generally purchased from publishers who offer discounts and replacement plans, though other titles may be purchased to supplement the variety of the collection and to meet patron requests.
- Unabridged titles are purchased with few exceptions.
- Donations of titles by popular authors are added if in good condition.
- Very popular titles on cassette are replaced on cd as they are weeded.

WEEDING

- The collection of books on CD is growing; weeding is mainly by attrition. More space becomes available to them as cassettes are removed from the collection. We will watch trends to determine when the collection has reached its ideal size or has been superseded by a new technology.

GOALS

- Relative use and active use statistics indicate that the collection is considerably smaller than desirable. However, technology changes quickly and we will need to monitor how long to build this collection and when funds should be transferred to a new format.
- We have a growing collection of MP3 disc audiobooks which are donations from Recorded Books. We will monitor their popularity in deciding whether titles should also be purchased.

STATISTICS

	Relative Use	Active Use	Average Age	Turnover
CD Book	5.81	97%	3.2	7.4
Audiocassette	0.77	57%	10.5	5.2

DVDs and DVD-TVs

DESCRIPTION

This collection consists of two sections of DVDs: feature films (including wide-release documentaries), and popular television series.

PHILOSOPHY

The feature film section of the DVDs was begun in 2001 and has been developed as a deep collection encompassing the entire history of film-making. Films from every era and every genre have been added to the collection with the intention of providing examples of the full range of the filmmakers' art for our patrons. This addition of "old" movies has proven to be important now that most of the video stores in the area have closed down. "New" movies are added based on popularity at the theater, on quality within their genre, and on awards (such as the Academy Award). The television section was begun in 2011 and is still developing. While building the collection, the focus is on currently popular series, with the intention of filling in with "classic" television programs.

SELECTION

- DVDs are located for these two sections by examining patron holds (particularly High Demand Holds); by reading movie and television reviews in newspapers and magazines; by checking the charts of highest grossing films and most watched television shows; and by reading magazines on popular culture such as *Entertainment Weekly.*

- Priority is given to purchasing current films and television shows first, with remaining funds used for patron requests and "classic" titles.
- Donations of DVDs in good condition are highly encouraged for each section, with duplicates of high demand titles held in reserve as future replacement copies.

WEEDING

- Damaged titles will be considered for repair or replacement if warranted by their circulation statistics.
- In the future, circulation statistics will be the main criteria for weeding this collection.

GOALS

- The DVD collection is still growing and shows extremely high demand by all statistical counting methods.
- In the future new formats, such as Blu-Ray, will be added as demand increases.

STATISTICS

	Relative Use	Active Use	Average Age	Turnover
DVD	13.62	100%	4	16
TV-DVD	10.33	98%	2.3	11.5

VHS

DESCRIPTION

The Library has a small circulating collection of VHS tapes for titles that may not be readily available on DVD.

PHILOSOPHY

VHS format has been replaced by DVD for almost all titles. The Library retains copies of nonfiction titles on VHS, in particular geographical and historical series.

SELECTION
- Selectors will not add new VHS titles.
- Selectors should review whether titles currently held on VHS are now available on DVD.

WEEDING
- Selectors should review the VHS tapes for wear and condition after 100 circulations. VHS tapes should be weeded after two years without circulating, unless they represent significant local or historical interest.

GOALS
- This collection should be phased out by the end of 2015.

STATISTICS

Relative Use	Active Use	Average Age	Turnover
0.35	37%	9.8	0.8

Music CDs

DESCRIPTION
This section consists of recorded CDs, primarily music but also a small number of spoken-word discs. The collection was begun in the late 1980s as a mostly classical collection, but other music styles were added in earnest beginning in the early 1990s to meet growing patron interest.

PHILOSOPHY
This is an extremely popular collection. Due to space and budget constraints, supply does not meet demand. Adult and Young Adult titles are shelved together, though each department selects its own materials to meet individual needs. An effort is made in the adult collection to purchase popular and classical music of the widest variety to meet the entertainment and educational needs of the community.

SELECTION

- Popular magazines and library journals, "hit lists," radio playlists such as Sirius XM, and music websites such as http://allmusic.com are utilized.
- The adult collection purchases "uncut" or "uncensored" items when a choice is required.
- Due to budget, packaging and shelving constraints, "boxed sets" are not purchased.
- We receive many excellent donations of music CDs and select many of them to supplement our collection.

WEEDING

- Weeding is mostly by attrition. This is a growing collection, but some allowances must be made for space. Fortunately, high circulation assists with shelving issues.
- Replacement is necessarily high due to theft of materials.
- Out of print items are not replaced. We do not purchase used CDs.

GOALS

- This collection is still growing. Due to its popularity according to relative use and active use statistics, space and budget are the biggest considerations as to collection size.

STATISTICS

Relative Use	Active Use	Average Age	Turnover
4.63	92%	7.2	5.4

Adult Kits

DESCRIPTION

This section consists of CD and DVD kits of educational materials by the Great Courses Company. The courses cover a wide variety subjects in history, science and the arts.

PHILOSOPHY

Our small collection has developed strictly through donations of used copies of the materials. Though they are popular with a small group of patrons, due to their high cost and relatively low local interest we have chosen not to purchase them.

SELECTION

- We add donated copies of Great Courses sets when available. Hanging kit bags are purchased to house the sets, which may include booklets, audio CDs, and/or DVDs.
- Our subscription to the Universal Class database may eventually eliminate our need to house this donated collection of educational courses.

WEEDING

- Weeding is by attrition, as materials are lost or damaged. Some individual titles comprise two or more kit bags, and all are withdrawn if any of the parts is unusable.
- Two shelves are dedicated to the kits; titles may be weeded in the future based on space needs.

GOALS

- The adult kits collection can be maintained at its current size. New titles are added very occasionally as they are donated, and kits are weeded at approximately the same rate. If patron interest in this sort of collection grows, we might consider purchasing titles, though active marketing of the Universal Class database would likely fulfill most needs.

STATISTICS

Relative Use	Active Use	Average Age	Turnover
2.93	N/A	4.8	3.3

E-Readers

DESCRIPTION
The La Grange Public Library currently owns four Sony Readers and three Barnes & Noble Nook Colors. One copy of each device is held at the Reference Desk to assist patrons, and the rest of the copies circulate to the public.

PHILOSOPHY
In 2011, using funds from the Friends of the Library, we first purchased e-readers to circulate to the public. We purchased over 20 e-books for each device in order for patrons to become familiar with reading e-books.

SELECTION
- The Sony Reader was selected for its durability and compatibility with Media on Demand. The Nook Color provides full color illustrations for children's picture books, adult cookbooks and travel guides.
- Library staff members are conducting patron surveys in 2011 and 2012 to determine patron interest in different e-reader formats, such as the Amazon Kindle.

WEEDING
- All the circulating e-readers have extended warranties, and they can be replaced if damaged.

GOALS
- As this is a new collection, we need to determine which devices are of interest to our patrons, and to purchase new devices when funding is available.
- In the future, e-reader devices may become less popular as tablets become less expensive. We will explore circulating tablets to the public.

STATISTICS

Relative Use	Active Use	Average Age	Turnover
N/A	0.71%	0.5	36.2

Video Games

DESCRIPTION

- The video game collection consists of games for four different con-soles: Nintendo DS, Nintendo Wii, Xbox 360, and PlayStation3.
- We acquire games of all ratings that have an intended teen and adult audience, and all games rated T (teen) or above are in the adult collection.
- Games with characters from the Disney, Mario, Sonic, and LEGO series are all kept in Youth Services, unless a rating is unsuitable for children.

PHILOSOPHY

We decided to circulate video games after doing an in-house survey of patrons in 2009 asking them if they would check video games out and if so, which console. The top three were the DS, Wii, and Xbox 360 by a wide margin. The Friends of the Library donated money for the opening day collection, and the management team decided to focus the collection on offering a variety of popular titles.

SELECTION

- The website www.metacritic.com is a great resource to find video game reviews.
- Currently, circulation statistics show the Xbox 360 is the most popular format followed by Wii and then DS. Buy *at least* two Xbox 360 and Wii games for every DS game. The same titles may be ordered for multiple consoles, but reviews vary for each con-sole version.
- We will purchase popular games for the PlayStation3 if they are exclusive to this console.

- Currently, music and sports games circulate the most for Wii, shooter and racing games circulate the most on Xbox 360, and puzzle games circulate the most on the DS. It is important to provide a variety of genres for each console.
- Because of the cost of each game, we rarely purchase duplicates, and especially do not duplicate titles available in the Youth Services collection.

WEEDING

- Games should be withdrawn when they no longer work or have not circulated in one year.

GOALS

- This is a growing collection with very high relative use, active use, and turnover statistics. We should explore patron interest in purchasing additional formats, such as Nintendo 3DS.

STATISTICS

Relative Use	Active Use	Average Age	Turnover
12.64	99%	1.5	13.0

Magazines

DESCRIPTION

The Library collects magazines for adults, young adults, and children. Adult magazines are stored in the Quiet Reading Room, young adult magazines are on wall shelving in the YA room, and children's magazines are shelved in the YS room.

PHILOSOPHY

We will keep a variety of subject areas, so the collection will be broad enough to appeal to as many patrons as possible. The adult magazines cover pop culture, home and garden, cooking, finance, and news. The YA magazines focus on fashion, sports, design, music, humor, news, gaming, and writing, published with a target audience of 12–18 years old. The YS magazines cover parenting, comics, sports and creative play.

SELECTION

- Patrons and staff are encouraged to recommend titles to add to the collection.
- The title is reviewed by all adult selectors and they vote whether to add the title.
- Magazines are added based on their topic's interest level in the community.

WEEDING

- We withdraw titles from the collection when they cease publication.
- Subscriptions may also be cancelled by selectors due to low in-house statistics (done twice per year), lack of circulation, and rising subscription fees.
- Using the LGPLMagRenew blog, a renewal list is sent monthly to selectors so they can review the previous year and current prices, to determine whether the title should be renewed.

GOALS

- Re-assess the space needs and circulation of the magazine collection, in particular the retention of issues (i.e., two years). Continue to evaluate titles as they are renewed.

STATISTICS

	Relative Use	Active Use	Average Age	Turnover
Adult	0.84	46%	1.6	1.1
YA	0.56	37%	1.4	0.5
YS	0.60	43%	1.4	0.8

Berkshire Athenaeum (MA)
Weeding Policy and Procedures (January 2010)

*The full document is available online at www.pittsfieldlibrary.org/policy_
weeding.html.*

BERKSHIRE ATHENAEUM IS the library serving Pittsfield, MA. It serves
a population of 44,737 (2010 census). The Weeding Policy and Procedures section of their Collection Development/Maintenance Policy does
a marvelous job of looking at each Dewey section, giving direction and
general guidance for each section of the collection. The policy also spells
out a schedule for weeding.

Weeding Policy and Procedures
Collection Development/Maintenance Policy

1. Policy Overview
Weeding the collections is as vital to the health of the Berkshire Athenaeum as adding new titles. Each item, through its quality, reliability,
current usefulness and appearance, must earn its place on the shelf, and
contribute to the reliability, reputation and attractiveness of the Library.
Systematic weeding is an integral part of book selection, pointing out the
weaknesses of the collection.

2. Responsibility for the Collection
Final authority for the determination of the policies in this document
are vested in the Library's Board of Trustees. They have delegated the

responsibility of implementing this policy to the Library Director. The Library Director may delegate to specific staff members the responsibility for withdrawal of materials in certain specific areas, but recommendations of these staff members are always subject to review by the Director.

It is the function of librarians to select and to withdraw library materials and to advise on their use. Recognizing that sensitivity to the needs and interests of the community is essential to the development of library collections, the Athenaeum welcomes advice and suggestions from the community, trustees and authorities in various fields. Librarians, however, are responsible for judging the needs of their collection and community, and they must make the final choices.

Weeding should be done without bias by individuals, whose personal preferences or interests will not dominate their work. Librarians are expected to include in the collection, when available, materials that reflect all sides of controversial questions.

3. Weeding Criteria

3.1. GENERAL CONSIDERATIONS: Every title requires individual judgment. Each item is considered from the standpoint of its value to the community as well as in relation to other items on the shelf. Materials are candidates for weeding if they are factually inaccurate, worn or damaged and beyond mending or rebinding, superseded by a truly new edition or a much better book on the subject, of no discernible literary or scientific merit, unused, and/or are irrelevant to the needs or interests of the Pittsfield community. Duplicate titles no longer in demand should be withdrawn. Duplicate formats will not necessarily be retained. The availability of materials through the interlibrary loan network allows books items of limited appeal to be weeded and space given to more useful material; and some collection areas, especially those of a more technical nature, will be weeded more heavily as a result of content updates available on the Internet. The current bibliographies noted in the appendix to the

Library's materials selection policy (SELECTION BIBLIOGRAPHIES AND REVIEW SOURCES) will be consulted prior to withdrawal.

The following sections, roughly divided by Dewey Classification range, will show a special coding in the form of a ratio. These formulas are intended as broad guidelines only, and the Athenaeum recognizes there will be many exceptions to these "rules." The first number refers to the age of the material, or the number of years since the item's latest copyright date. The second number refers to the maximum number of years without usage. An "X" in the place of a number indicates that no clear default number of years is applicable.

3.2. 000 (GENERAL): The availability of online resources for general information look-ups makes encyclopedia sets less a core resource than previously; therefore these sets are purchased on a staggered schedule, generally with the intent of being able to offer one relatively new set (less than 3 years old) at any given time. The shelf life for materials in this range is generally good for about five years, unless they are specialized and very dated items, like almanacs and computer guides, which are good for two years.

3.3. 100 (PHILOSOPHY AND PSYCHOLOGY): (10/5) Collection should keep abreast of popular topics in psychology. The value of materials on philosophy is determined mainly by use.

3.4. 200 (RELIGION AND MYTHOLOGY): (10/5) The collection should have something up to date on each religion represented by a church, synagogue, or other assembly in the Pittsfield area, provided such materials are available. Generally the shelf life for items in this range is ten years except for areas of rapid change.

3.5. 300 (SOCIAL SCIENCES): (10/3) Books on government and economics should be replaced by new editions as available. Unless they have an historical approach they are of little use after ten years. Books on finance, opportunities for wage earners, college guides, career guides, and educational testing are outdated sooner. Books on customs and etiquette may have a longer shelf life depending on whether the subject matter is consistent with current ideas. Books on folklore may be kept well beyond ten years, depending on condition.

3.6. 400 (LINGUISTICS AND LANGUAGE): (10/5) Need only stock dictionaries and grammar instruction for languages being (or likely to be) studied or spoken in Pittsfield.

3.7. 500 (PURE SCIENCES): (10/3) Mathematics, general biology, natural history and botany have a shelf life of ten years, but other sciences may be dated much sooner as new research supersedes earlier data. Basic works of significant historical or literary value, such as Darwin's *Origin of Species* should be kept indefinitely.

3.8. 600 (APPLIED SCIENCES AND TECHNOLOGY): (7/3) Technology is making such rapid advances that material over seven years old should be viewed with suspicion with obvious exceptions. Repair manuals for older cars and appliances should be retained as long as such items are generally used in Pittsfield. Books on clocks, guns and toys may be kept beyond ten years since such items are often collectable. Cookbooks, unless unused, also enjoy a much longer shelf life. Books on Medicine (except anatomy and physiology) and home economics become dated much sooner as style and technique change rapidly.

3.9. 700 (ARTS AND RECREATION): This range generally enjoys a relatively long shelf life, and most items may be kept, especially histories of art and music, until worn and unattractive. Books on crafts (X/3) may be retained if they contain basic technique and the illustrations are not too dated. Books on photography (7/3) should be checked for outdated technique and equipment. Books on sports (7/3) should be weeded if they deal with personalities no longer of interest.

3.10. 800 (LITERATURE): (X/X) Keep basic materials, especially criticism of classic writers. Discard works of writers no longer read or discussed in literary histories (such as poetry, drama, essays or letters). Discard minor writers no longer read in area schools, unless there is an established demand among non-students. Keep literary histories unless they are superseded by better titles.

3.11. 900 (HISTORY AND GEOGRAPHY): (15/3) Books on history generally enjoy a longer shelf life than most of the collection. The main factors include demand, accuracy of facts, and fairness of interpretation. Personal narratives and war memoirs of World War II, the Korean War, and the Indochina Wars may be weeded in favor of broader histories of these conflicts, unless the author is a local person, or the book is cited in a bibliography as outstanding in style or insight. Dated viewpoints should be discarded. Books on travel (4/2) become dated much more rapidly, however personal narratives of travel (10/3) enjoy a somewhat longer shelf life, especially if they are of high literary or historical value. All local material and accounts in which local people have participated should be kept.

3.12. BIOGRAPHY: (X/3) These books are shelved separately in the Children's, Young Adult and Adult collections. Unless the person treated is of permanent interest or importance, biographies may be weeded as demand stops. This applies especially to ghost written biographies of faddish celebrities. Poor quality biographies of major celebrities should be replaced with better ones if funds permit. Biographies of outstanding literary value are to be kept until worn, without regard to the biographee's reputation.

3.13. ADULT FICTION: (X/3) Discard works no longer popular, especially second and third copies or old best sellers. Retain works of durable demand or high literary—merit good, non-topical, well-written novels appealing to universal concerns will continue to circulate for many years.

3.14. LARGE PRINT: (X/3)

3.15. MASS MARKET PAPERBACK: (X/1)

3.16. CHILDREN'S FICTION: (X/3) Discard books where the format and reading level are no longer appropriate to the current interest level of the book; topical fiction on dated subjects; abridged or simplified classics to be replaced by the original; second and third copies of series books no longer popular.

3.17. CHILDREN'S NON-FICTION: Use the same criteria as adult but looking especially for inaccuracy and triviality, the more common faults of over simplified children's nonfiction.

3.18. YOUNG ADULT FICTION: Use the same criteria as Children's fiction.

3.19. YOUNG ADULT NON-FICTION: Use the same criteria as Adult non-fiction.

3.20. PERIODICALS: (5/X) Microfilm copies of heavy demand magazines and newspapers useful for research are acquired. Because of space restrictions, back files of magazines are generally no more than five years, and newspapers are kept generally no more than several weeks. Exceptions to this practice include magazines in the fields of genealogy, local history, environmental science, social commentary, religious commentary and opinion which may be retained in longer runs as necessary in response to demand. Standard news magazines (i.e., NEWSWEEK, TIME AND U.S. NEWS AND WORLD REPORT) are retained indefinitely, as are a number of unique titles (i.e., AMERICAN HERITAGE, LIFE, and NATIONAL GEOGRAPHIC).

3.21. LOCAL DOCUMENT REPOSITORY: These documents by design cover issues with widely varying life spans in local interest and impact. Although consideration will be given to the possible long-term historical importance of these documents, the Athenaeum cannot and will not provide a permanent archive of the materials. All documents accepted for the public information repository are accepted with the understanding that the Reference Department will determine when these documents will be deaccessioned. Criteria for this decision will include the amount of use the document received, the currency and local relevance of the issue it concerns, the available library space, the format of the materials, and the local availability of the information at another location. The Athenaeum will make no attempt to return documents to the agency of origin.

3.22. AUDIO VISUALS: (X/3) Worn out or damaged, rarely used, trivial and faddish are the general criteria taken into consideration when weeding audio visual items. VHS and cassette recordings are weeded somewhat more aggressively given that these are media the library no longer is supporting through further acquisitions.

3.23. SCORES: (X/3) Condition and missing parts are the primary considerations when weeding scores. The availability of multiple copies and the popularity of the work are also contributing factors.

3.24. LOCAL HISTORY DEPARTMENT: Because of the very specialized nature of this collection, it is dealt with separately in the LOCAL HISTORY DEPARTMENT: COLLECTION DEVELOPMENT POLICY STATEMENT.

4. Frequency of Weeding

Weeding should not be a major project undertaken once every several years or when there is no longer room to shelve the materials. The collection as a whole should be reviewed systematically. One section at a time, each book should be considered individually, keeping in mind the general selection criteria and the terms in the above section on weeding criteria. Some sections will require more frequent review than others. The following chart will serve as a very broad guideline for the frequency each section should be reviewed.

Collection/Years Between

DEWEY RANGE	SYSTEMATIC REVIEW
000	3
100	4
200	5
300	3
400	5
500	2
600	2
700	3
800	5
900	4
Biography	2
Fiction	2
Large Print	2
Paperbacks	1
Children's	2
Young Adult	3
Scores	5
AV	2

5. Disposal

5.1. SELL: Most books discarded from the library are sold through the periodic Friends of the Berkshire Athenaeum book sales.

5.2. RECYCLE: While not as "profitable" as selling the items, this option can generate the best public relations when discarded materials are passed along to other agencies (i.e., libraries, schools, day care providers, nursing homes, social service providers, jail, third world countries, etc.).

5.3. DESTROY: Generally reserved for the worst books that no one wants or would buy at the book sales, while this option requires the least effort, it can generate bad public relations because readers may be shocked that the library would throw away "good books."

5.4 REQUESTS FOR PURCHASE: Occasionally the Athenaeum will receive a request from a reader to be given the opportunity to purchase or otherwise acquire a book or item from the library's collection when that item is withdrawn. Because of the volume of materials the library must handle it is unreasonable to assume library employees can track such requests, nor will such requests impact the library's decision whether an item should be withdrawn. Persons making such requests are advised to periodically check the periodic Friends of the Library used book sales.

Memorial Hall Library (MA)
Collection Development Manual (2014)

The full document is available online at www.mhl.org/about/policies/ cd/#h3_16.

MEMORIAL HALL LIBRARY, in Andover, Massachusetts, serves a population of 34,000. Their collection development manual is wonderfully thorough, with details on how and why items are selected. There are specific sections on replacing items, mending items, and a General Weeding Policy, which are reprinted here.

Replacement Copies

FORMAT	IDENTIFY TITLES FOR REPLACEMENT	REPLACE IF:
Books	Printouts for long overdue or lost items are checked in database to determine number of copies, number of circulations, publication date Mending shelf is checked for candidates for discard and repurchase Reserve lists and ILL requests are checked for replacement candidates Reference librarians make suggestions for replacement for items that "should be" available but aren't New or updated edition is available	Book is still in demand and is in print, and we don't have adequate copies of the title, or sufficient subject information in other books Try hard to replace "classic" titles Be sure to keep adequate number of titles of items continually in demand New edition has substantially updated information

FORMAT	IDENTIFY TITLES FOR REPLACEMENT	REPLACE IF:
Audio-books	Long overdue or lost items Visual inspection of collection Patron identified items that are in poor condition Periodic checks of circulations on high circulating/shabby looking items	Title is still in demand Replace single CDs where appropriate Repurchase entire title, either from same vendor or another vendor if entire set is past its useful life Most titles are not replaced
DVDs	Long overdue or lost items Staff or patron identified items that are in poor condition	DVD is still in demand and not dated
Music CDs	Long overdue or lost items Damaged items	Title is still in demand Replace "classic" titles

General Weeding Policy

Reasons for Weeding

- To identify and withdraw incorrect or outdated materials. Users are dependent on us to provide up-to-date information. Outdated medical, legal, travel, tax and educational information especially can cause serious problems for our users.
- To remove from the collection those materials no longer being used. If the collection is full of materials that are not being used, our users cannot find the materials that they do want. Last year we added approximately 18,500 items and withdrew 12,000 items. Optimally, shelves should not be more than 3/4 full, with the top and bottom shelves empty as they are hard to reach.
- To remove worn or damaged materials. Attractive, clean materials are preferred by users and give the message that the library is a modern, up-to-date source of information. A well maintained col-

lection sends the message that we expect users to treat our materials with respect and return them in the good condition in which they were borrowed. Users appreciate a well maintained collection and are more likely to support it with their tax dollars than they would support a library collection that looks like someone's old attic. Popular worn titles should be withdrawn and replaced with attractive newer editions. Classics will circulate well if they are clean and inviting.

- To increase circulation. Paradoxically, decreasing the size of the collection often results in increasing circulation. Users find it difficult to find useful materials when the collection is overcrowded with outdated, unattractive, irrelevant materials. Weeding makes the "good stuff" more accessible. Death from overcrowding is a common result of collections that are not properly and regularly weeded.

The Weeding Process

1. Identify items that are candidates for weeding:

   - Library pages and aides remove shabby, outdated materials for consideration by the professional librarian.
   - Menders set aside poor candidates for mending for consideration by the professional librarian. Replace if appropriate.
   - Library pages and aides use printouts of items not circulated in a certain amount of time (generally one to three years, depending upon subject, genre, collection or format) to remove items for consideration by the professional librarian. Where appropriate, aides and pages will note if there are other copies of the book, or other books on the subject on the shelf.
   - Examine (as per the weeding guidelines outlined in this manual) specific date sensitive areas, e.g., travel guides, science, medicine, law, and technology, and weed those items whose information is not current.

- Weed subject areas where currency is less urgent, less often, but still on a regular basis, based on computer generated usage statistics and condition.
- Encourage all professional staff to be on the alert for dated and superfluous materials. Expect staff to make suggestions for weeding and replacement on a continuing basis, for all areas of the collection, both print and nonprint.

2. Physically prepare items to be withdrawn.
3. Remove items from the database.
4. Order replacement titles as necessary.

Collection Formats—Adult Collection

All Collections

COLLECTION/ FORMAT/CLASS	ACQUISITION GUIDELINES	WEEDING GUIDELINES
	Consider selecting library materials in all formats available for adults Buy bestsellers, works by popular authors and high demand items Buy multiple copies as budget allows of popular materials and items in demand	Continuously weed using last activity date and number of circulations since date of acquisition Identify worn items still in demand and mend or discard

Print Collections

COLLECTION/ FORMAT/CLASS	ACQUISITION GUIDELINES	WEEDING GUIDELINES
All Print Collections	Generally, buy one copy per four reserves of items in demand Consider buying multiple copies of classics still in demand Buy heavily for new book displays Buy multiple copies for school assignments, if needed	Generally weed materials that have not circulated in one to three years Weed classics by condition and replace with new, attractive editions
Fiction	Buy general fiction, mysteries, science fiction, short stories and graphic novels Buy hardcover editions for general fiction and consider buying duplicate copies of trade paperback editions for popular titles/authors (if available) Buy series titles we own if still circulating and do not buy series titles we don't own, unless in high demand	Weed multiple copies when demand ebbs
Large Print	Buy multiple copies of best-sellers if budget allows	
Books-To-Go	Buy multiple copies of best-sellers Buy hardcover editions for Books-To-Go, trade paperbacks for Notable Books-To-Go	Weed duplicates once demand ebbs
Paperbacks	Buy mass market copies of popular books	Weed by condition and generally do not replace or mend
Book Club	Buy trade paperbacks of popular books	Weed frequently by condition

Print Collections

COLLECTION/ FORMAT/CLASS	ACQUISITION GUIDELINES	WEEDING GUIDELINES
Notable Books	Buy trade paperbacks of prize-winners	Weed by condition and space limitations
Nonfiction	Buy a broad range of nonfiction subjects, especially in the most popular subjects, i.e., cooking, health, self-help, house and garden, crafts, personal finance and biography Be careful not to buy well reviewed titles that may be too academic for library patrons Buy textbooks only in math and science Use standing order plans for annual publications, such as test preps, travel, and popular tax and legal publications	Weed more frequently books that date quickly
Periodicals and Newspapers	Buy a wide variety of subjects and viewpoints for adults of all ages Consider whether available online in full text Continuously check for new publications as titles come and go, asking staff for suggestions Consider multiple copies of popular subscriptions Buy duplicate copies of the highest circulating titles for our Mags-to-Stay collection Consider patron requests	Check circulation statistics for last few years for titles up for renewal and renew based on usage Consider price per potential usage Ask circulation staff and pages about usage in the library

Audiovisual Collections

COLLECTION/ FORMAT/CLASS	ACQUISITION GUIDELINES	WEEDING GUIDELINES
Audiobooks	Buy fiction, mysteries, science fiction, short stories, biographies and general nonfiction Buy popular authors, bestsellers and high demand titles Select based on demand, quality of writing, narrative voice and style, appropriateness for audio format, and enhancement of text Buy unabridged fiction Buy mostly unabridged versions of nonfiction unless book is overlong or only abridged version is available	Weed by condition and use Replace individual tapes if feasible
Foreign Language CDs	Buy language CDs for beginners and advance speakers Buy multiple copies of in demand languages	Replace dated language CDs with newer materials
Playaways	Use standing order plan for popular authors/bestsellers	

Audiovisual Collections

COLLECTION/ FORMAT/CLASS	ACQUISITION GUIDELINES	WEEDING GUIDELINES
DVDs, Quick Flicks	Buy feature films, television series/shows, foreign films, independent films, music/ opera, how-to videos and documentaries Buy feature films at release date Buy new, well-reviewed and/or popular films Add classics as budget allows Buy up-to-date travel DVDs for popular destinations Buy multiple copies of new titles (Quick Flicks) that can't be requested or renewed	Weed by condition as DVDs have a tough time holding up to library circulation Keep one copy of Quick Flick title for replacement
Music CDs, CDs-To-Go	Buy classical and nonclassical music Buy in all genres, styles, time periods, composers and performers Buy duplicates of in-demand items Buy new, popular titles for CDs-To-Go collection	Weed by condition and use Replace high demand items May add CDs-To-Go to our regular collection
CD-ROMs	Buy for genealogy and local history	Weed by condition

Mixed Media Collections

COLLECTION/ FORMAT/CLASS	ACQUISITION GUIDELINES	WEEDING GUIDELINES
Chinese and Russian Materials	Buy books, magazines, newspapers, DVDs, CDs Buy popular, in-demand items Buy music classics, folk songs and popular artists	Weed by condition and usage Analyze usage of magazines
English as a Second Language (ESL)	Buy materials for new readers and persons speaking English as a second language Buy language programs in DVD and CD formats Buy high interest/low vocabulary materials	Weed by condition and usage

Digital Media Collections

COLLECTION/ FORMAT/CLASS	ACQUISITION GUIDELINES	WEEDING GUIDELINES
E-Book/eAudio	Buy best sellers and high demand items, same as print media For fiction buy general fiction, mysteries and science fiction For nonfiction buy popular subjects, such as biographies and self-help Use same selection criteria as audio-books Buy multiple copies of popular items	
Electronic Resources/ Streaming Media	Considerations include: authoritative-ness, timeliness and accuracy, quality and uniqueness of information, target audience, depth of coverage, easy to use interface, price, vendor reputation, customer support, and advantage over comparable print resource	

Collection Formats—Young Adult Collection

All Young Adult Collections

COLLECTION/ FORMAT/CLASS	ACQUISITION GUIDELINES	WEEDING GUIDELINES
	Buy in most formats for middle school and high school audience (grades 6–12)	Continuously weed
	Buy popular, in-demand items	Replace worn items still in demand
	Consider buying all works by bestselling authors/artists	

Young Adult Print Collections

COLLECTION/ FORMAT/CLASS	ACQUISITION GUIDELINES	WEEDING GUIDELINES
Fiction	Limit collection to popular authors and those books that are highly recommended	Weed heavily in the fall
Nonfiction	Buy recreational, informational and educational books Buy heavily in areas for student research, i.e., countries, social issues Watch for additions to series Add revised editions when available.	
Paperbacks	Primarily a browsing collection of contemporary and classic fiction and recreational nonfiction Buy additional copies for summer reading titles and popular authors	Weed and replace often
Graphic Novels and Manga	Select well-reviewed novels that appeal to teens Watch for new additions to series	
Magazines	Subscribe to a wide variety of magazines, both general interest and specialized	Discard after 1 year

Young Adult Audiovisual Collections

COLLECTION/ FORMAT/CLASS	ACQUISITION GUIDELINES	WEEDING GUIDELINES
Audiobooks	Buy recordings of well-reviewed young adult books Occasionally purchase classic titles	
Music CDs	Buy mostly music that's in demand with frequent air play, both popular and alternative	Important to check for last activity date
Video Games	Buy video games for a variety of current consoles	

Young Adult Digital Media

COLLECTION/ FORMAT/CLASS	ACQUISITION GUIDELINES	WEEDING GUIDELINES
E-books— Overdrive	Select popular titles using same selection criteria as other formats	

Collection Formats—Children's Collection

All Children's Collections

COLLECTION/ FORMAT/CLASS	ACQUISITION GUIDELINES	WEEDING GUIDELINES
	Buy through grade 6 Buy materials to support homeschoolers Buy popular, in-demand items Consider buying all works by bestselling authors/artists	Continuously weed all sections for condition and shelving space Replace worn items still in demand Add revised editions of popular items, when available

Children's Print Collections

COLLECTION/ FORMAT/CLASS	ACQUISITION GUIDELINES	WEEDING GUIDELINES
Board Books	Heavily used by infants and toddlers	
Picture Books	Buy broadly Buy multiple copies for standard and popular titles Buy multiple copies in paperback for titles in demand Buy books on a variety of cultures	
Beginning Readers	Buy heavily and in multiples Replace old editions with reissues in color Continue to build leveled collections as they become available Buy "hot" titles for kids (characters, such as, Batman, Scooby Doo, Disney, etc.)	

Children's Print Collections

COLLECTION/ FORMAT/CLASS	ACQUISITION GUIDELINES	WEEDING GUIDELINES
Younger Fiction	Commonly called "Bridge Books," these beginning chapter books for transitional readers are in demand Buy multiple copies of popular authors and series Buy backup paperbacks in quantity Buy additional titles on summer reading lists and MCBA (MA Children's Book Awards)	
General Fiction	Retain and replace classics and "modern" classics Buy genres such as mysteries, fantasy, science fiction and ghost stories In general, buy one copy with backups of popular titles in paperback Buy additional titles on summer reading lists and MCBA	
Graphic Novels	Buy more titles	
All nonfiction	Use the Core Curriculum to buy well-reviewed trade titles and multiple copies of high demand topics Watch for additions to well established series	
300s	Buy fairy tales and folklore, especially from other countries and cultures	Weed Christmas books
400s	Build foreign language holdings (both instructional materials and materials in other languages), especially Spanish, French, Russian and Asian languages	

Children's Print Collections

COLLECTION/ FORMAT/CLASS	ACQUISITION GUIDELINES	WEEDING GUIDELINES
500s	Maintain currency of science titles on a variety of levels Many good science experiment books only available in paperback Buy books on space, planets, and the solar system to update and support summer reading Use STEM (Science, Technology, Engineering and Math) guidelines	Weed astronomy, planets and solar system
600s	Buy health material appropriate to various age levels through 6th grade Buy other applied sciences as available Use STEM guidelines	Weed space travel and technology
700s	Buy heavily for arts, crafts, sports Buy for wide variety of ages and interests	
800s	Buy short story and poetry collections as available Buy plays and skits Buy multiple copies of popular titles	
900s	Maintain current information on countries and states Maintain backup reference material Buy heavily: early civilizations, American history, medieval and modern history Buy three copies each of well-used series	

Children's Print Collections

COLLECTION/ FORMAT/CLASS	ACQUISITION GUIDELINES	WEEDING GUIDELINES
Biography	Buy heavily for readers in all grades Buy for various grade levels: explorers, artists, scientists, athletes African-American biographies are in great demand Buy paperbacks as well as hardcovers Useful for less well-known figures	
Collective Biography	Use Collective Biography Index for possible titles Buy when good series are available	

Children's Audiovisual Collections

COLLECTION/ FORMAT/CLASS	ACQUISITION GUIDELINES	WEEDING GUIDELINES
DVDs	Maintain balance of educational and entertainment titles	Weed and replace continuously with new titles
Music CDs/ Audiobooks/ Playaways/ Puzzles	Maintain as a browsing collection Important to keep in good working order and add to as appropriate material becomes available	Weed continuously for condition and replace with new titles
Litkits	Developed for day care and preschool use Develop kits on new topics as budget allows	Refurbish as needed
E-Books	Select popular children's titles through Overdrive using same selection criteria as other formats	Check circulation statistics after 6 months and decide whether or not to continue buying this format
Electronic Resources	Continuously evaluate online resources for purchase	

Glen Ellyn Public Library (IL)
Collection Development Policy, Procedures, and Plan

The full document is available at: http://gepl.org/about/policies/
collection-development-policy

THE GLEN ELLYN Policy, Procedures, and Plan document clearly lays out every section of materials selection and briefly describes the goals of collecting in each Dewey area. There are separate sections for various formats as well as a separate Youth policy. The Retention and Weeding and Roles of the Collection portions are reprinted here.

Retention and Weeding

Retention and weeding in all areas of the library will be focused on retaining those materials and resources that meet the needs of the Glen Ellyn community.

Retention of print or electronic materials is based on the likelihood of a historical interest in the field as well as the timeliness of a title and its informational content. Member demand also has an impact on the retention or replacement of materials.

Weeding of print or electronic materials is done on an ongoing basis as needed. Weeding criteria for both print and electronic materials will be currency and demand for the subject matter. The physical condition of heavily used print materials will also be a consideration.

An essential consideration in retention of online database products is Member use. A subscription database that does not show substantial use considering the cost of the product over a time period of a year or more will be replaced or removed.

Titles of newspapers and magazines are kept for varying lengths of time, depending on space. The Glen Ellyn News is kept on microfilm dating back to 1912.

Roles of the Collection

The collections of the Glen Ellyn Library serve the following purposes:

- Education support for high school through adult learners
- Popular materials center
- Reference library
- Education Support Center

The collection's educational role is to support formal education from high school through adult independent learning. In addition, some material may be collected for Members for whom English is a new language (ENL) as determined by the community's changing demographics.

Selectors will bear in mind the needs of students, particularly recurring assignments, in developing the collections. However, high school and college textbooks will generally not be purchased. The Library does keep a separate, non-circulating collection of textbooks provided by local schools. These are donated by the schools and the Library requests updates as needed.

In order to meet the needs of adult independent learners, the collections will provide a broad range of information in all subject areas. A basic selection of the principal works in each subject area and of classic fiction also will be maintained.

Interlibrary loan service will be provided on request to supply most professional and academic level titles for which there is no general demand.

Popular Materials Center

Popular materials are those which are in demand by the community. Selectors will take into consideration demand as reflected by reserve/ purchase requests and may consult community groups or subject experts regarding special needs for materials in specific subject areas.

Multiple copies will be purchased in various formats to meet Member demand. After initial demand has passed, most duplicate copies will be removed from the collection, due to lack of space.

Reference Library

A general collection of reference sources for use only inside the library will be maintained. The reference collection will cover all disciplines at a basic level and in a variety of formats. Where available, an encyclopedia or general overview and appropriate periodical indexes will be maintained in each broad subject area. The Library will provide electronic access to information which is most easily searched in that format.

Due to the nature of reference material, the reference collection cannot be comprehensive. More in-depth research materials can be found at the local academic libraries.

Reference materials which are in high demand and require extended use may be duplicated in the circulating collection.

A small collection of local history materials is maintained as Reference material. In general, questions of this nature are referred to the Glen Ellyn Historical Society.

Specific Book Collections

Reference Collection

The availability of information on the Internet has increased our library's access to timely information, necessitating a smaller more select print reference collection. This collection serves the general Member; thus, we do not have an extensive legal, tax or medical information appropriate for professionals practicing in these areas. The Reference Collection is continuously updated.

Fiction

The Fiction collection encompasses general fiction, mysteries, and science fiction. Well-reviewed titles are given a priority. The replacement of tattered copies of classic fiction will be an ongoing expenditure. The majority of fiction purchases will be hardbound, but paperbound copies may be purchased as replacements. Every attempt is made to acquire and maintain books in a series written by a popular author. The number of copies purchased of popular fiction will be based on demand. Once an individual title is no longer popular the library will reduce the number of copies of that title.

Non-Fiction Circulating Collection

The non-fiction collection of the Glen Ellyn Public Library is classified in the Dewey Decimal System and uses Library of Congress Subject Headings. Additional copies of popular nonfiction will be purchased based on demand. Once an individual title is no longer popular, the library will reduce the number of copies of that title.

000—Generalities

Areas of special emphasis include:

Computer Science and the Internet, Journalism and Publishing, Reader's Advisory: The computer book collection will address the needs of home computer users. Some titles on older software applications are kept, but the bulk of this section is devoted to newer software titles that are currently in widespread use.

100—Philosophy and Psychology

Special emphasis will be placed on self-help materials and topics in demand for school assignments.

200—Religion

The collection will include a general overview of each of the major world religions. Mythologies of the world will be covered on a basic level.

300—Social Sciences
Areas of special emphasis in the social sciences include:

- College guides/Test Prep; Finance/investment; Legal guides; True Crime.

Current information is crucial in most of these areas. Tax guides are kept for 7 years. Multiple copies are weeded after the current tax year.

400—Language
The collection will include English grammar, usage, and etymological materials; a dictionary and grammar book for each major language; and materials meant for Members for whom English is a new language.

The English as a New Language (ENL) collection does include some textbooks and workbooks. This is a developing collection and will be periodically evaluated to ensure that it meets the needs of the Glen Ellyn community.

500—Science
This collection will include books on natural history, mathematics and pure sciences for the layperson.

An emphasis is placed on materials for students, high school through basic college. This is another area where the library does purchase some textbooks, since they are frequently the best source for well-written overviews on physics, mathematics, astronomy, etc.

600—Applied Science and Technology
Areas of special emphasis in the 600s include:

- Health/specific diseases; gardening; cooking (including special diets and ethnic cuisines); business/jobs; parenting; home construction projects.

The subject area of medicine will consist of lay level books on specific diseases, systems of the body, and health encyclopedias.

700—Arts
Areas of special emphasis in the arts include:

- Hobbies and Crafts; Interior design and home decoration; Architecture; Performing Arts; Sports.

800—Literature
The collection will cover world literature on a basic level. Special emphasis will be placed on the following:

- Shakespeare plays and criticism; Drama; Criticism of works and authors; Poetry; Essays; Humor.

910-919—Travel
This collection will cover all areas of the world, with emphasis on major international and United States cities. Multiple copies of popular travel guides will be purchased.

900—History, Biography
Special consideration is made to balance the needs of students as well as the interests of those who simply enjoy reading history. The collection includes books on local history as well as basic books on genealogy.

Biographies
Biographies commonly found at the classification number 920 will be separated out into their own section. Biographies and autobiographies of single individuals are here, with the exception of sports celebrities and artists, which will be found in the 700s. Biographies about more than one person are usually classified in the most appropriate Dewey area. The titles are classified by the name of the subject of the book.

Large Print
Large Print titles are usually duplicates of popular interest titles held in the other collections, both fiction and non-fiction.

Adult Mass Market Paperbacks

The mass market paperback collection is meant as a non-comprehensive, rotating collection of current, popular interest titles, including genre fiction. Only fiction will be purchased in mass market paperback format. Tattered copies with high circulation will be replaced.

Graphic Novels

The Graphic Novel collection consists of fiction and nonfiction titles in pictorial form using text and sequential art to tell the story. Preference is given to hardcover titles, although paperbacks will be purchased when that is the only available format. Selection criteria are the same as above but also include the quality of graphics.

Young Adult/Teens

The Library will maintain a collection of fiction and non-fiction books which appeal primarily to young people of high school age. The collection will include some classics commonly read in high school but will be primarily a browsing collection of popular materials for this age group. Every effort will be made to acquire books on local school reading lists. Age and interest-appropriate Graphic Novels will also be purchased for this collection. When appropriate, books will be purchased in paperback format.

Newspapers and Magazines

The Newspapers and Magazine collection consists of approximately 250 titles, including reference serials. The collection includes popular titles in a broad range of subject areas.

Databases and Electronic Resources

The electronic collection will reflect the academic needs of students at the junior high level through college, as well as the reference needs of the general public.

When feasible, electronic sources are made available from remote locations as well as inside the library.

Audiovisual Materials and Resources

The library will continue to expand its collection of audiovisual formats. As new technologies emerge, older formats will be phased out, depending on Member demand. Shelving and storage options also have an impact on these collections.

Seattle Public Library
Weeding Instructions for Branch Libraries

THE SEATTLE PUBLIC Library consists of a Central location and twenty-six branches. The branches have roughly one million items, and this in-house document covers general details for weeding in the branches.

Following the branch document is another internal document used at the Central location, the Reader's Services Department Weeding Guidelines.

General Weeding Instructions for Branch Libraries

Principles and Practicalities
The Seattle Public Library withdraws worn, damaged and outdated materials to offer our patrons a collection that is credible, useful, timely and attractively displayed. Presenting an attractive and engaging collection of resources, avoiding overcrowded shelves and hard to reach areas (top and bottom shelves) are all important to the vitality and usability of our branch collections. As part of a system, each branch relies on the greater system collection to meet the needs of patrons.

When to Weed
Weeding is an essential, ongoing assignment in collection development and maintenance. If this activity is deferred or only given cursory attention, weeding activity will need to be focused and intensive until the collection is brought to system-wide standards with shelves no more than 2/3 full, top and bottom shelves are empty. Once the collection meets the

standards, it can usually be maintained with a regular schedule. A lot can be accomplished in 20-30 minutes a day or a couple of hours each week. The important goal is that the activity is routine, regular and ongoing.

Getting Started

Because of the range of building capacities, layouts, and shelf arrangements in our 26 locations, each branch has its own challenges and rewards. As a general retention practice, smaller branches (2,000-5,000 square feet) may consider retaining most volumes for up to 2 years, medium branches (6,000-10,000) 2-3 years and larger branches (over 10,000) for 3-5 years—assuming condition and currency of information are sound.

- Step One: Pull for condition.
- Step Two: Pull for date (especially in the areas of consumer health, law, finance and cover-dated materials such as tax guides, etc.).
- Step Three: Pull superseded editions such as travel guides, job readiness resources and annual issues.
- Step Four: Once these steps are completed, then request dusty shelf as the fourth step. "Dusty Shelf" reports are useful for identifying underused resources in a library collection. However, these reports do not identify worn or outdated volumes which are the materials that have the most negative impact on the collection's credibility and the patron's experience. For that reason, dusty reports should always be the fourth step in comprehensive weeding activity.

Apply these general principles for all formats:

1. *Physical Condition:* Materials that are worn, damaged, or soiled are considered unfit for circulation. Faded and unattractive buckram rebinds, yellow, brittle or torn pages or marked pages, missing pages and illustrations (no "Officially Noted" stamps, please) are all marks of poor physical condition. Media items with missing components including cover art, librettos and booklets should be withdrawn. Items in this category can be withdrawn

wherever they are encountered. It is NOT necessary to return damaged items to their assigned locations for withdrawal.

2. *Timeliness:* Out-of-date materials undermine the Library's credibility and, in some subject areas, can cause serious harm. Dated materials are worse than nothing, not better than nothing. Patrons expect and need up-to-date materials, particularly in the areas of travel, consumer health, and personal investing—all areas that are regularly updated through publishing output and selection activity.

3. *Superseded Editions:* Retain only the current edition of regularly updated materials such as travel, study guides, consumer legal guides, tax manuals, resume guides, etc. Note: Reference items on standing order should not be transferred to the circulating collection when a new edition is received. The superseded edition should be withdrawn.

4. *Duplicate Copies:* Multiple copies are purchased when titles are at peak popularity. Once the excitement subsides, duplicate copies on the shelf consume valuable and scarce real estate. Trim to a single copy or withdraw all copies and rely on the holdings of Central and the larger branches.

5. *Low Circulation:* Withdraw items that have not circulated in a year or show a steady decline in circulation.

6. *System-Wide Holdings:* Remember that we are a system of libraries with one collection shelved in multiple locations. If your copy is showing wear and tear or space is at a premium, relying on the larger collection is legitimate and necessary.

Withdrawal Procedures

Most withdrawn volumes and media items in good condition should be directed to the Friends of the Library. Please follow the withdrawal procedures available on InfoNET. Additional information about de-processing items prepared by the Friends of the Library is also on InfoNet.

As most branches are at or near capacity and all branches are actively engaged in collection maintenance activities, surplus copies should not be offered to other branches.

Reassigns

All branches are at or have exceeded LFA-identified shelving capacity leaving only the Central Library with space to accept reassigns. Some 55,000 items were absorbed by Central as part of the Mobile Integration in 2011 leaving some areas of Central strained. TCS will consider reassigning items not needed in your collection if the item is in new or like-new condition and the item is absent at Central or in lost or missing status. Media items should be complete, in good playable condition and with inserts, jacket and librettos intact. Search Horizon before sending items to TCS for reassign consideration. If there are multiple copies on the shelf at locations across the system, consider your copy surplus and send the withdrawal to the Friends of the Library.

Instructions for using the gray reassign slip for sending items to TCS for reassign consideration are available on InfoNET. While the Central Library is not a designated "last copy" repository, the last system copy owned of a title will be considered for reassign to Central if it is judged to have continuing merit and is in satisfactory condition. Indicate "last copy" on the grey reassign slip.

Seattle Public Library: Reader's Services Department Weeding Guidelines, Rev. 9/20/12

Priorities for weeding: (in priority order)

1. *Condition*: Watch for curling or chewed up covers, yellowed or torn pages, stains, burn marks and other patron markings, smelly or moldy items, missing pages, broken bindings and worn, dirty and ugly bindings. Also, pull all the books needing new plastic jackets or spine labels. We mend mass paperbacks only if they can be fixed with ONE piece of tape.
2. *Circulation*: Even unpopular titles at Central have circulated between 12–20 times. However, if an item hasn't circulated in the past 12–18 months, ask yourself why we should keep it. A Dusty Shelf List report gives you an easy way to start your mending.

3. *Duplicates*: Central often receives two or more copies of a new title. Sometimes one copy will suffice, if circulation is low. Weed popular title duplicates down to between 3–4 copies.

4. *Series books when most titles are missing*: TCS views ALL of SPL as one library, so no one branch, including Central, will own an entire series, except in rare instances. When you see one mid-series title on the shelf, it's a good idea to check the series and see if a) we have other series titles, b) if the series needs to be read in order, 3) if so, do we have in our branch the first one or two of the series and the most recent, and 4) if it's a well-written and important series we need to keep. Branches owning other series titles may find a better use for a singles series entry languishing on the shelves.

5. *Out-of-date older titles*: Most popular older titles are worn out or in new editions and are easily identified as of enduring value. Sometimes, however, a pristine-looking older title is really just a shelf-sitter. Be careful as you read titles/authors on the shelves. If you don't recognize them as current or important older titles/authors, pull them and check.

6. *Obscure authors or authors in less demand*: Dead authors who wrote just one book, authors who used to be popular whose books are not circulating anymore, and authors you don't recognize should all be carefully considered for discard/retention. While we have an interest in collecting local authors, we may discard local titles if they do not meet our criteria for retention (above #1–5). You may wish to consult another librarian to support your decision.

7. *Ephemeral titles*: These can be books purchased because the author is local, but are poorly written or no longer of interest to our community, tiny books that were funny for a while but not anymore, mass market paperbacks of one unknown author languishing on the shelf, oversize books that don't look like fiction or look like children's books and unknown books with mediocre shelf appeal.

8. *Last copies* may be discarded when they do not meet our standards.

9. If you can't decide whether or not to discard a book, weigh in favor of discard if it has an "Obsolete" RFid tag.
10. Our goal is to keep our collection weeded to its space, meaning empty bottom shelves and each shelf filled to 75%.

These are priorities to think about as you look at the shelves and anything you wonder about should be pulled for evaluation. If you know the books you pull will sit on your desk/cart for a while, change the item status to "CM" (collection maintenance). If you decide to keep it, remember to check it in! Items sent to menders must have "ME" status. Once mending is done, the librarian judges the quality of the mending and checks in the ones fit for public shelving.

Questions to ask before discarding a book in good condition, but with low circulation:

1. Is it a book we "should" have such as a classic, a well-known author or first in a popular series?
2. Is the book one that would be of interest in our community if publicized?
3. Is it by a Seattle or Northwest author? Is it still of interest to our community?
4. Does the author have other titles at SPL that do circulate well?
5. Has the book been readily available for checkout? Did it come to CEN from another library (MOB) recently? Has it been shelved on the top or worse, bottom shelf?

Columbia University (NY)

Collection Development Policies

The full document available online at http://library.columbia.edu/about/
policies/collection-development.html.

HAVING A SIMPLE, general statement covering how the library handles weeding and discarding is an easy and smart option. The full collection development plan covers the selection areas individually in depth but does not mention timeframes or guidelines for weeding. The "Preservation Policy" and "Weeding and Discard Policy" are reprinted here.

Preservation Policy

The responsibility to build research collections carries with it the obligation to ensure that these collections are permanently accessible. The Columbia University Libraries is committed to the preservation of its collections. Preservation is the action taken to prevent, stop, or retard deterioration of all library materials in all media; to prevent their theft or loss; where possible to improve their condition; and, as necessary and appropriate, to change their format in order to preserve their intellectual content.

The comprehensive approach to preservation entails choosing the most appropriate method of preservation for every item. This is accomplished through storage of materials in proper conditions, through careful handling and housing, through use of security systems designed to eliminate mutilation and theft, through refreshment and migration of electronic files, and through repair or replacement of damaged materials. Materials of unique aesthetic or historical value should be preserved in their original form. There are many other materials whose value lies primarily, or only, in the information they contain. When repair of such materials becomes impossible or prohibitively expensive, their content may be preserved through reformatting into other media. The indefinite storage of unusable materials within the Libraries cannot be justified.

Columbia, as a research library, selects most materials for permanent value. Some materials, however, may not be a permanent part of the collection because they are of only short-term interest to scholars. Department and distinctive collection librarians and selection officers are responsible for developing and maintaining a collection which meets the needs of their library users. Therefore, preservation decisions for materials in the collections is best determined by these officers in consultation with each other, the Preservation Division, reference staff, and others including the faculty when necessary. Preservation decisions must always be made within the context of overall collection policy, balancing the constraints of cost, historical and aesthetic and scholarly value, and user accessibility.

Weeding and Discard Policy

Decisions to discard specific items, like decisions to acquire new titles for the collection, are made within the context of the total collection policy, so that the integrity of the total collection is not impaired but in fact may be enhanced when unneeded materials are removed from the collections. Materials identified for discard in one library are first made available to other units of the University libraries; if there is no interest at this level, these materials may be used for exchange with other institutions, sold to students or dealers, given to other libraries, or in some other way applied to the University's benefit. In some instances, materials may be so deteriorated or otherwise useless that disposal through any of the above channels is not possible; such materials may simply be discarded.

Emmanuel d'Alzon Library, Assumption College
Collection Development and Retention Policy (Worcester, MA)

The full document is available online at www.assumption.edu/sites/default/ files/library/pdfs/Coll_Dev_Policy_8-13.pdf.

THE COLLECTION DEVELOPMENT and Retention Policy for the Emmanuel d'Alzon Library is notable because it describes specific procedures for staff to use to develop the library collection. The policy details a number of guidelines for selection, and includes the following text to guide staff in weeding and retention:

Review Process for Evaluating Books in the Collection

Members of the faculty are encouraged to review books in their respective subject areas and to bring books that should be removed from the collection to the attention of the appropriate subject liaison. After a liaison has determined that items are not exempted by the repository standards enumerated above, the liaison is expected to bring items to cataloging staff or other designated librarians to be removed from the collection.

Nonetheless, it is recognized that many members of the faculty do not have time to locate and examine materials that are shelved in their normal locations. For that reason, the appropriate subject liaison or designate is expected to evaluate the collection on an ongoing basis. The chair of the appropriate department should be notified that items have been selected for possible removal from the library collection. Members of the faculty should have a minimum of two weeks to look at such items to determine if they warrant removal or if they should be returned to the collection. If a librarian other than the subject liaison has designated materials for review, the liaison will be notified to review the selections to make a similar determination. As appropriate, library workers will be notified to return designated materials to their normal locations in the library collection.

After the stated time has passed, items that remain under review will be removed from the collection.

Criteria for Evaluating Books

- Incomplete sets should be considered for removal unless:
  - Remaining volume(s) in the collection make(s) sense on a stand alone basis, or
  - Replacement of missing volume(s) is feasible.

- An item in obviously poor condition should be removed unless:
  - Removing the work would create a significant gap in the collection, and
  - Replacing the work would cost more than $50. If the work can be replaced for under $50, staff time would be better spent focusing on the repair of more expensive items. A work that meets both criteria above should be transferred to the repair shelves, unless the work would be removed under other criteria without regard to condition of the item.

- Duplicate copies of works over ten years old should be removed unless:
  - Each copy has circulated at least once during the past three years, or
  - The work is of a general nature, such as an introductory retrospective work.

- Multiple editions of works should be reviewed for removal if later editions are acquired.
- Materials should be considered for removal if they are in a language not actively taught at Assumption College unless they contain significant information (e.g., art reproductions).
- Works pertaining to current technologies or health sciences that are more than five years old should be considered for removal unless they contain significant retrospective or historical information.

Evaluating the Reference Collection

Under the direction of the Head of Reference, Reference Librarians evaluate the collection on an ongoing basis. In addition to using the DUSTIE Guideline books are evaluated to see if they could be more useful to our patrons if they were transferred to the circulating collection. Frequent weeding or transferring is needed to avoid overcrowding of the space allotted for the collection. Subject liaisons are notified when works are designated for review and they are expected to evaluate the usefulness of such items for the circulating collection, using the criteria for the subject areas involved. After decisions have been made, the cataloging staff processes the items for transfer to the circulating collection or for removal from the collection, as appropriate.

Baltimore County Public Schools
Selection Criteria for School Library Media Center Collections

*The full document is available online at https://bcpslis.pbworks.com/w/file/
fetch/68240711/CollectionDevelopmentSelectionCriteria.pdf.*

THE BALTIMORE COUNTY Public Schools Selection Criteria for School Library Media Center Collections is a full collection development policy, and the sections on assessing and weeding collections are reprinted here.

Assessment and Inventory Process

An essential step in collection development is assessment of the needs of the curriculum and student population with regard to library media resources. Library media specialists will develop yearly and long-range plans to assist in ongoing assessment.

Assessment of the collection includes taking inventory of existing materials, assessing materials in relation to needs of instructional units, and weeding outdated and inappropriate materials.

The inventory is a process by which holdings are checked against the automated cataloging system and the actual item to determine if the resource is still part of the collection and still meets selection criteria. The objective of this inventory is to ensure that the automated cataloging system accurately reflects the collection which is the key access point for students and teachers to locate information within the library.

This procedure should not disrupt the library media program as automation of school library holdings greatly speed up the process using the barcode scanning feature. An annual inventory is recommended as the data is critical to making collection development decisions about the quality and quantity of the collection in meeting the needs of students and staff.

Inventory Procedures

Weeding Library Media Materials

A good collection development plan must include weeding. The process of weeding is a key part of assessing the collection. It helps keep collections relevant, accurate, and useful; and it facilitates more effective use of space in the library media center.

Library media materials should be weeded if they:

- Are in poor physical condition
- Have not been circulated in the last five years
- Are outdated in content, use, or accuracy (Copyright date should be considered; however, do not make a decision to weed based solely on the copyright date of the material. Some older material may be considered classic or may be of great historical value to your collection.)
- Are mediocre or poor in quality
- Are biased or portray stereotypes
- Are inappropriate in reading level
- Duplicate information which is no longer in heavy demand
- Are superseded by new or revised information
- Are outdated and unattractive format, design, graphics, and illustrations
- Contain information which is inaccessible because they lack a table of contents, adequate indexing, and searching capabilities
- Are not selected in accordance with general selection criteria

Withdrawing Library Media Materials

Although the final decision to withdraw materials from the library media collection is one which is made by the library media specialist, subject area, grade level teachers, and other faculty members may be invited to review the items marked for withdrawal.

All withdrawn materials must be sent to the Pulaski Warehouse/Distribution Center for recycling. Withdrawn materials should not be sent to classrooms; the same standard of quality applies to all other instructional materials within the school.

SUGGESTED READING

Articles and Books

Albitz, Becky, Christine Avery, and Diane Zabel, eds. *Rethinking Collection Development and Management.* Denver: Libraries Unlimited, 2014.

Baumbach, Donna J., and Linda L. Miller. *Less Is More: A Practical Guide to Weeding School Library Collections.* Chicago: American Library Association, 2006.

Dickinson, Gail. "Crying Over Spilled Milk." *Library Media Connection* 23, no. 7 (2005): 24–26. www.linworth.com/pdf/lmc/reviews_and_articles/featured_articles/Dickinson_April_May2005.pdf.

Doll, Carol Ann, and Pamela Petrick Barron. *Managing and Analyzing Your Collection: A Practical Guide for Small Libraries and School Media Centers.* Chicago: American Library Association, 2002.

Gregory, Vicki L. *Collection Development and Management for 21st Century Library Collections: An Introduction.* New York: Neal-Schuman, 2011.

Greiner, Tony, and Bob Cooper. *Analyzing Library Collection Use with Excel®.* Chicago: American Library Association, 2007.

Gwinnett County Public Library. *Weeding Manual.* 2nd ed. Gwinnet, GA: 2002; distributed by the Public Library Association.

Hibner, Holly, and Mary Kelly. *Making a Collection Count: A Holistic Approach to Library Collection Management.* Oxford: Chandos Publishing, 2010.

Hoffman, Frank, and Richard Wood. *Library Collection Development Policies: Academic, Public, and Special Libraries.* Lanham, MD: Scarecrow Press, 2005.

Jacob, Merle. "Weeding the Fiction Collection: Or, Should I Dump Peyton Place?" *Reference & User Services Quarterly* 40, no. 3 (2001): 234–9.

Johnson, Peggy. *Fundamentals of Collection Development and Management.* 3rd ed. Chicago: American Library Association, 2014.

Larson, Jeanette. *CREW: A Weeding Manual for Modern Libraries, Revised and Updated.* Austin, TX: Texas State Library and Archives Commission, 2012. https://www.tsl.state.tx.us/ld/pubs/crew/.

Saricks, Joyce. "The Lessons of Weeding." *Booklist,* September 1, 2011. www.booklistonline.com/At-Leisure-with-Joyce-Saricks-The -Lessons-of-Weeding-Joyce-Saricks/pid=4994130.

Singer, Carol A. *Fundamentals of Managing Reference Collections.* Chicago: American Library Association, 2012.

Sloate, Stanley J. *Weeding Library Collections: Library Weeding Methods.* 4th ed. Englewood, CO: Libraries Unlimited, 1997.

Vnuk, Rebecca. "Weeding Tips" series of features on *Booklist Online.* To access the full run of columns, visit www.booklistonline.com and search for "Weeding Tips."

Websites

"Book Weeding." Milwaukee School of Engineering's page devoted to the topic of weeding at the library. www.msoe.edu/community/campus-life/ library/page/2012/book-weeding.

Holley, Robert. "Maximizing Revenue from Selling Withdrawn Books and Unwanted Gifts." October 27, 2010. YouTube video, from an ALCTS Webinar. https://www.youtube.com/watch?v=J94q1w1Dx2M.

"Space, Space, Space: Weeding and What Remains." University of California, Irvine Libraries' website on their weeding project. http://libguides .lib.uci.edu/fiatfluxweeding.

"Workbook for Selection Policy Writing." Office for Intellectual Freedom of the American Library Association. www.ala.org/bbooks/ challengedmaterials/preparation/workbook-selection-policy-writing.

"Weeding." Arizona State Library, Archives and Public Records. Collection Development Training. http://apps.azlibrary.gov/cdt/weeding.aspx.

"WesWeeding." Wesleyan University Library's weeding project site. http:// weeding.blogs.wesleyan.edu.

INDEX